THE
FIELD&STREAM
Deer Hunting Handbook

The *Field & Stream* Fishing and Hunting Library

HUNTING

The Field & Stream *Bowhunting Handbook* by Bob Robb

The Field & Stream *Deer Hunting Handbook* by Jerome B. Robinson

The Field & Stream *Firearms Safety Handbook* by Doug Painter

The Field & Stream *Shooting Sports Handbook* by Thomas McIntyre

The Field & Stream *Turkey Hunting Handbook* by Philip Bourjaily

The Field & Stream *Upland Bird Hunting Handbook* by Bill Tarrant

FISHING

The Field & Stream *Baits and Rigs Handbook* by C. Boyd Pfeiffer

The Field & Stream *Bass Fishing Handbook* by Mark Sosin and Bill Dance

The Field & Stream *Fish Finding Handbook* by Leonard M. Wright, Jr.

The Field & Stream *Fishing Knots Handbook* by Peter Owen

The Field & Stream *Fly Fishing Handbook* by Leonard M. Wright, Jr.

The Field & Stream *Tackle Care and Repair Handbook* by C. Boyd Pfeiffer

THE
FIELD&STREAM
Deer Hunting
Handbook

Jerome B. Robinson

Illustrated by Christopher J. Seubert

THE LYONS PRESS

Copyright © 1999 by Jerome B. Robinson

Illustrations by Christopher J. Seubert

All rights reserved. No part of this book may be reproduced in any manner whatsoever without the express written consent of the publisher, except in the case of brief excerpts in critical reviews and articles. All inquiries should be addressed to: The Lyons Press, 123 West 18 Street, New York, NY 10011.

Printed in the United States of America

10 9 8 7 6 5 4 3 2 1

Library of Congress Cataloging-in-Publication Data

Robinson, Jerome B.
    The field & stream deer hunting handbook / Jerome B. Robinson; illustrated by Christopher J. Seubert.
        p.   cm. — (Field & stream fishing and hunting library)
    Includes index.
    ISBN 1-55821-911-0
    1. Deer hunting   I. Field and stream.   II. Title.   III. Title: Field and stream deer hunting handbook.   IV Title: Deer hunting handbook.   V. Series.
SK301.R635   1999
799.2'765—dc21   98-43471
                                                                    CIP

Contents

Acknowledgments   vii

1 Whitetail Distribution and Density   1

2 Big Buck Country—How to Find It, How to Get There   7

3 The Art of Seeing Deer   11

4 What Deer Tracks Tell You   17

5 How Weather Affects Whitetails   24

6 How to Dress for Deer Hunting   31

7 The Rut: Buck Behavior and How to Take Advantage of It   34

8 Hunting in Groups   40

9 Hunting from Stands   45

10 What Is Still-Hunting, and How Do You Do It?   51

11 When to Use Scents   55

12 Deer Calls and How to Use Them   58

13 Rattling Antlers for Big Bucks   62

14 Use of Map and Compass   70

15 Firearms and Cartridge Choices   76

16 Rifle Sights   80

17 Sighting-in Your Rifle   84

18 Picking Your Target: Where to Shoot a Deer   89

19 Trailing Wounded Deer   93

20 Field Dressing Your Deer   98

21 Dragging Your Deer Home   102

22 Firearms Safety   105
23 Hunting Gear Checklist   107
24 Favorite Venison Recipes   108
   Index   113

Acknowledgments

I am indebted to a legion of successful hunters, guides, and wildlife biologists who have instructed me in the ways of the whitetail during more than 30 years of writing on deer-related subjects.

Too numerous to mention by name, these experts have shared their knowledge, methods, and hunting skills. This book relays the essential information they have passed along.

Being a successful hunter means more than just getting a deer. Successful deer hunters succeed because they have learned to hunt well. The intention of this book is to teach you how to hunt well, too.

If you use the information contained here, success will follow.

THE
FIELD & STREAM
Deer Hunting
Handbook

CHAPTER 1

Whitetail Distribution and Density

THE WHITETAIL DEER is the most abundant big-game species in North America. Thanks to modern scientific management and effective law enforcement, the whitetail population of the lower 48 states has leaped from roughly 500,000 to perhaps 25 million in the past century. Hunters now harvest an annual crop of approximately 6 million whitetail deer.

Despite their abundance, mature whitetail bucks are rarely easy to find once hunting season is under way. Whitetails are among the most secretive, elusive, and canny animals that roam the countryside. Hunting them successfully is one of the greatest challenges North American hunters can undertake.

Hunters who manage to take deer season after season aren't just lucky they succeed because they have learned more about deer behavior than other hunters, and they have developed hunting skills that others lack. The aim of this book is to teach you what you need to know in order to join the ranks of those consistently successful deer hunters.

BALANCING THE POPULATION

In each state the wildlife department is responsible for keeping the deer population in the state balanced at a number the natural habitat can sustain into the future. The deer-carrying capacity of a region is determined by forestry and agricultural practices, which affect the availability of nutritious food at the low point of the winter food shortage period. The carrying capacity is then reviewed in the light of how much deer-related damage the public can be expected to accept in the form of agricultural crop losses, forest depletion, damage to landscape shrubbery, and highway accidents caused by deer. Subsequently, hunting regulations are established that can be expected to generate sufficient harvests to keep deer-related damages within acceptable limits, while still maintaining deer in numbers that will satisfy hunters.

Hunters who consistently take big whitetails generally know more about deer behavior and have developed skills that others lack.

By removing antlerless deer from the population, hunters are helping wildlife managers maintain the deer herd at its optimum level.

Since one mature buck will mate with many different females, the most effective way to reduce a deer population that is in danger of exceeding the carrying capacity of its range or is causing unacceptable damage is to increase the harvest of does through hunting. Removing females lowers the deer population's reproductive rate and effectively reduces the number of young deer that will be added to the overall herd.

ANTLERLESS SEASONS

When states establish special antlerless seasons in specific areas, the intent is to encourage hunters to take females for the long-range good of the local deer population. It is also important to remove females from certain deer populations in order to maintain a balanced ratio of bucks to does. In regions where hunting pressure is heavy, regulations that permit hunters to take only bucks soon lead to skewed populations in which antlered deer are rare and antlerless deer are overabundant.

Sometimes state efforts to reduce the number of antlerless deer are met with hunters' disapproval. It is important, however, for deer hunters to understand the importance of limiting the number of antlerless deer in order to increase the ratio of mature bucks within a given population. Hunters who fail to recognize the significance of keeping deer herds in balance may refuse to shoot does, saying they would rather see more deer, not less. Too often the result of this stubbornness is large-scale deer starvation when top-heavy antlerless deer populations exceed the biological carrying capacity of their range.

Don't let anyone tell you "it's not sporting to shoot does." In areas where doe seasons have been in effect for several years, does have become extremely wary and alert and are every bit as challenging to hunt as bucks.

DOE HARVESTING HELPS

Because of the general increase in deer populations, most regions now offer hunters the opportunity to take deer of either sex. Hunters should understand that by removing antlerless deer from the population when permitted to do so, they are helping wildlife managers maintain the deer herd at its optimum level and are improving the opportunity for bucks within that population to grow to maturity.

In states where deer populations have been kept within the carrying capacity of their range and a high percentage of bucks reach maturity, it is not uncommon for bucks to attain very large body size, often exceeding 200 pounds field-dressed. In general, the largest deer live in northern latitudes because large body mass is protection against winter's low temperatures, whereas the smallest deer are found in southern latitudes where winter temperatures are less stressful. The weight of mature does is generally about 75 percent that of mature bucks.

ANTLER DEVELOPMENT

Antlers are an adornment that grow after all other nutritional needs have been met. So, when deer populations are kept within the carrying capacity of their range and all herd members have adequate nutritious food year round, antler development increases and trophy racks become more common.

Antlers are an adornment that grows after all other nutritional needs have been met. Antler development increases when deer populations are kept within the carrying capacity of their range.

In well-managed deer ranges it is not uncommon for 2½-year- old bucks to carry 8-point racks measuring more than 15 inches. Where the deer population exceeds the optimum carrying capacity of its range, however, bucks may require an additional year to produce antlers of equivalent size. In poor, overcrowded ranges, bucks may never develop trophy racks.

DOMINANT BUCKS

Bucks that attain the greatest weight and the largest antlers dominate smaller bucks and usually succeed in breeding most of the does within their home range. However, the effort of fighting other bucks in order to retain dominance, plus the stress of breeding large numbers of does, takes its toll. Dominant bucks frequently have shorter lifespans than females and subdominant bucks.

Thanks to scientific management, deer populations are now being maintained at optimum levels throughout most forests and farmlands in North America. For the hunter, that means there are more excellent deer-hunting opportunities today than ever. Furthermore, the educated deer hunter is the primary tool that managers rely on to keep deer populations within acceptable limits.

Big Buck Country—
How to Find It,
How to Get There

BIG BUCKS are older bucks, and they don't attain maturity by making mistakes. Consequently, the biggest bucks are usually the most difficult to find, and the areas in which they seek refuge are exactly where hunters are least likely to be encountered.

Where hunting pressure is high, mature bucks retreat during daytime hours to places where their experience has taught them that people do not go. They head for mountain ridges, plunge deep into swamps, lose themselves in the middle of huge fields of standing corn, or seek the cover of brushy river bottoms. If you want to find big buck country, examine your hunting territory and ask yourself where you would go if you were an old buck that did not want company. Then go there yourself. Go quietly and move slowly. Stop often to sit and watch. Look for large deer droppings, large deer tracks, ground scrapes, and rubs on trees where a buck has polished his antlers. Watch, too, for large, single deer beds.

As you assemble these bits of information, you will be defining the area a big buck uses. Eventually, you will have enough information to identify spots that offer good views of places the buck uses frequently. Those are the places you should hunt.

CROSSING WATER

Much of big-buck country that is difficult to reach from a road can be accessed by using a boat and crossing water. I frequently use a canoe or other small boat to cross a river or a lake to reach sections of deer country that are otherwise difficult to reach. Invariably, I find myself in big-buck country, and I usually have it all to myself because few deer hunters use boats.

When you're in remote country, move a few yards back into the woods along the shore of a lake or river. Chances are you'll find a well-beaten game trail that parallels the water's edge. That should tell you something about where deer move frequently.

Lake shores and river banks are natural boundaries in overlapping deer home ranges. Does and fawns amble along the waterways, browsing on the lush vegetation that grows in such places, and bucks patrol the same trails, often leaving their scrapes and rubs as evidence of their regular passage.

Wherever you can locate a section of lake shore or river bank in remote country that is not easily accessible from a road, you have discovered big-buck country. Not all big-buck country is remote, however.

WHERE THERE ARE DOES
THERE WILL BE BUCKS

I once hunted deer along a river in Wyoming and found plenty of good bucks living in brushy river-bottom cover that bordered on alfalfa fields within plain sight of ranch buildings and roads. Large numbers of antlerless deer could be seen grazing along the alfalfa edges at dusk and dawn, and we reasoned that with a good food supply and a doe herd available, there had to be big bucks nearby.

We used canoes to come down the river and hunted in the thick river-bottom brush on pieces of public land that were identified on our maps. Buck signs were everywhere, and six of us tagged heavy-antlered bucks in just two days. The bucks were not in remote country—it was just good deer country that was not being hunted because you needed a boat to reach it and most Wyoming deer hunters use horses, not boats, to reach their chosen hunting areas.

Using a small boat or canoe to cross water often gives you access to big-buck country that is hard to reach from the road.

Go Farther, Go Higher

Likewise, if you hike uphill until you reach a point where going any higher seems like too much effort, you have reached the point where most hunters turn back and big bucks begin to feel safe. Push yourself to go higher and you will enter big-buck country.

The edges of large forest swamps are used heavily by deer until they are disturbed by hunting pressure. Once disturbed, the big bucks move farther into the depths of the swamp where few hunters will pursue them. Going beyond the point where other hunters give up will put you in big-buck country once again.

Hunters who hang up big bucks consistently know where big bucks live and make the extra effort needed to hunt in those places.

Hunters who consistently hang up trophy bucks are usually in the woods earlier than most hunters, hunt farther back from roads, and stay deep in the woods until the end of legal shooting time. They know where big bucks live, and they make an extra effort to hunt in those places.

The Art of Seeing Deer

O NE OF THE SECRETS to successful deer hunting is learning to see deer before they see you.

The trick is to move slowly, stop often, and constantly study your entire view. That view changes every time you take a few steps, bringing new things into your angle of sight, so don't just plunge ahead thinking you have seen all there is to see. The coloration of deer blends into their surroundings, and their shapes are often broken up by the background, making the animals very hard to spot when they are still.

When looking for deer, don't look only for the shape of an entire deer—look for a piece of a deer. Learn to spot anything that seems out of the ordinary, and then study it. Rather than an entire deer, watch for the straight line of a back, the crook of an angled hind leg, the shape of an ear jutting out from behind a tree trunk, an antler moving slightly as a buck surveys his surroundings.

Learning to know where to look for deer is part of the challenge of hunting.

KNOWING WHERE TO LOOK

Remember that resting deer may be lying down with only their heads showing above a bulge in the ground or other obstruction. Often

Rather than looking for the entire deer, look for a piece of a deer. Learn to spot anything out of the ordinary, and then study it

Where is it looking? What is it looking at? A doe staring into the distance may be watching a buck that is traveling with her.

they will be bedded next to stumps, logs, and fallen branches that obscure their outlines, so check such places carefully. (Be sure to use binoculars for checking unknown objects; never your rifle's telescopic sight. You may be looking at a person, and your scope is mounted on a loaded firearm that is aimed at whatever you view through the scope.)

ARE THERE OTHER DEER NEARBY?

If you see a deer, freeze. Are there other deer nearby that you haven't seen? Sometimes you will be tipped off that more deer are in the vicinity by watching the attitude of the deer you have spotted. Where is it looking? What is it looking at? A doe staring into the distance may be watching a buck that is traveling with her.

Bucks sometimes travel in pairs or small groups of bucks of various sizes. Dominant bucks often have a subdominant buck or two tagging along with them. Thus, when you spot a buck with small antlers, don't assume it's alone. Stay still and watch. You may discover there is a larger buck with it.

UNFOCUS YOUR EYES

Sometimes it helps to "unfocus" your eyes when watching for deer. Your unfocused gaze will often pick up movement you might have missed if you were looking intently at one spot. When you are over-looking a broad reach of terrain, just keep your eyes open and slowly sweep your view. If something moves, your eyes will automatically zero in on that spot and you can determine what it was that caught your attention.

BE ALERT TO OTHER ANIMALS

While watching for deer, be alert to the movements of other animals and birds. Why is that blue jay squawking and flitting from treetop to treetop? Is it announcing that it sees something moving through the forest? What is that squirrel running from? Why did that crow swerve in flight? Did it notice something on the ground below? Learn to ask yourself these questions, and try to discover the answers. Sometimes you will discover a deer in the process.

On cold mornings, when your breath steams, watch for telltale plumes of vapor from the warm breath of a deer that may be hidden where you can't quite see it. Whenever you see an obscure deer-colored object, use your binoculars to check it for hair texture.

WATCH FOR SLIGHT MOVEMENTS

One frosty morning in Maine, I almost blundered into a big 8-point buck. He was completely hidden by vegetation in a thick clump of alders close to the bank of a north woods river. I had paused for a look around and suddenly noticed movement at ground level under the trees. I could see something small moving with a regular rhythm, but could not determine what it was. A grouse bobbing its head? It didn't look like that. A squirrel digging? I didn't think so.

I raised my binoculars and focused on the spot. The movement was a deer's hoof pawing the ground! Now I could see it clearly. The hoof would paw the ground several times, then stop, then a moment later paw again.

The deer's wet, black nose came into view as it sniffed the pawed place, its hot breath rising as steam. I still couldn't see the deer because its body was screened by vegetation, but the pawing action made me think *buck*. I kept the glasses focused on the spot, and the next time the deer lowered its nose to sniff the pawed place, I saw the tips of antlers catch the sunlight.

It was a buck, all right, and it was less than 100 yards ahead. I dropped to a sitting position and waited, watching. A breath of air moved through the forest from behind me, carrying my scent ahead. Suddenly, the buck caught my scent. He took a step forward, raised his head, and looked right at me. Now I could see him clearly. His entire head and neck and the forward part of his shoulder were in view.

He began to move as I raised my rifle, and as he turned broadside, I slid the crosshairs behind his shoulder and squeezed off a shot that dropped him in his tracks.

I went to his side, and as I was kneeling beside him admiring the heavy 8-point rack and rugged body, I noticed long, raking marks across his ribs and a bloody hole where an antler had punctured the base of his neck. Suddenly, I heard a buck utter a deep, guttural grunt from the other side of the alder clump. Another one! Now the raking scrapes and bloody puncture wound on my buck made sense. Before I came along and nearly walked into him, he had been fighting with another buck and had paused to paw the ground and work up his rage before returning to the battle.

I remained kneeling by my buck, watching. The other buck grunted again, so this time I made a soft grunt in reply. That was all it took. The buck came lunging through the thicket toward me, making all sorts of noises.

As he came into view, he apparently caught my scent mixed with that of the dead buck. He stopped short, then whirled and charged back the way he had come. But as he turned I got a good look at him, and he was magnificent. My big 8-pointer was no match for that buck. No wonder he had paused for a time out!

Checking a slight small movement had paid off for me that time. I saw the buck before he saw me, and I got a shot I would never have had if I hadn't frozen and studied what the woods were telling me.

CHAPTER

What Deer Tracks
Tell You

TRACKS TELL YOU the story of deer movement in your vicinity. If you learn to read tracks accurately, you will gain knowledge that can put you in a place where a buck wants to be.

Can you tell buck tracks from doe tracks? You can't always, but you can make a darned good guess according to the size of the track, the manner in which the hooves contact the ground, and where the tracks lead.

Size alone does not determine whether the track was made by a buck or doe. Plenty of big does have bigger feet than some bucks. But bucks and does place their feet on the ground differently, and they often travel by different routes, the combined information their tracks provide will give a strong indication of the maker's gender.

BUCKS CARRY WEIGHT FORWARD

Consider this: In autumn, mature bucks put on significant weight in their necks, which throws their balance forward so that they put more weight on their front feet than does do. This causes a buck's toes to spread as he walks and shifts his weight back onto the heels of his front hooves. The result is a distinctly different track, showing spread toes and dewclaws jabbed forcefully into the ground.

Thus, when you encounter a large, open-toed walking track with distinct dewclaw jabs at the heels, you should suspect that it was

In autumn, a mature buck leaves walking front-foot tracks that show spread toes, and its dewclaws jab forcefully into the ground because the buck carries his weight more on the heels of his front feet.

made by a mature buck. If there is snow on the ground and the tracks show long drag marks, indicating the deer barely raised its feet above the ground when walking, you can be even surer that you're looking at buck tracks. During the rut, bucks exhausted by the stress of breeding, fighting, and constantly searching for does drag their feet while walking, so their tracks sometimes look almost as if they were wearing skis.

Does show open toes and dewclaw jabs when trotting or running, but when they slow to a walk the toes close and the track becomes heart-shaped or takes the form of two straight slots with little or no dewclaw jab.

WHERE DOES THE TRACK GO?

Where the track goes will also tell a lot about who made it.

Does and little deer travel on established deer trails a great deal of the time. Bucks, however, have their own routes, which often cut across the bigger, heavily used deer trails. Bucks are often loners, so when you find the tracks of a large, single deer striking out over country, crossing the more heavily used deer trails and moving at a steady marching pace, you should suspect that the maker is a mature buck in the rut, striding cross-country in search of a doe in breeding condition, or estrus.

What happens to the track when it comes to a very low limb? Does usually duck under and continue on their way, but a heavily antlered buck has his rack to consider and usually goes around a low obstruction rather than under it to keep his antlers free.

READING THE SPOOR

When there is snow on the ground, pay particular attention to the sign left when deer pause to urinate. Females spread their hind feet slightly, and their urine falls from under their tail in a scattered, splash pattern between or on top of the hind tracks. Bucks, however, urinate from under their belly, and the steady stream of urine bores a clean hole in the snow somewhere between the front and hind tracks.

Droppings can also indicate the gender of the deer. When bucks are in the rut and on the move, they defecate while walking, scattering their droppings over 10 to 25 feet. Does, however, stop to defecate, and their droppings fall in a clump.

There is no mistaking the track of a really big buck. Medium-sized bucks are more difficult to distinguish from large does, but the indicators I've mentioned will help you tell buck tracks from doe tracks most of the time.

Aging Tracks

The condition of the track tells when it was made. Pay particular attention to changes in the weather, because it will affect tracks. If you know what time it started to rain or snow or what time the temperature dropped below freezing, you will be able to make an educated guess as to the age of a track. Was it made before or after the rain or snow began? Was it made before the ground began to freeze or after a skim of frost had formed?

Really fresh tracks made in deep snow are often filled with flakes that have fallen back into them, but you can determine their freshness by the condition of the crumbled snow around the edges. If it is very fresh, the snow around the edges will be rough and fluffy and have a bluish cast. As the track ages, the roughened snow around the edges is smoothed by moving air or sunshine. It loses its fluffy appearance and becomes grayish in color.

Fresh tracks made in soil also have loose crumbs around the edges that wear away with age. Tracks made in clay will retain clear definition until the next rain, but the roughness at the edges of a fresh track dries up and wears away within a few hours.

Feeling Tracks with Your Fingers

Tracks made in leaf litter are often indistinct to the eye, but you can learn a lot about them by pressing your first and second fingers into the track and feeling its shape and size. If the track is large, open-toed, and bearing heavy dewclaw jabs, you will be able to feel those characteristics and make an educated guess about the deer that made them.

When you first encounter a fresh set of large tracks, *do not* immediately bend over and start studying them. Instead, stand still and give your surroundings a long, hard scrutiny. The track maker may be within sight and may be looking back at you. The track will wait, and it should not be studied until after you have made certain that its maker is not nearby.

Fresh tracks are seductive. They make you want to follow them. But don't overlook what you can learn from older tracks.

Tracks made in leaf litter are often indistinct to the eye, but you can learn a lot about them by pressing your first and second fingers down into the track and feeling its shape and size.

LEARNING FROM OLDER TRACKS

Older tracks tell you the history of deer movement in your area. From them you can learn where deer travel most frequently, where they feed, and where they bed. Old tracks will lead you to rubs where bucks have polished their antlers and to scrapes where bucks have pawed the ground and left scent to attract does that are coming into estrus. With this information, you will have a much better idea of where you are most likely to encounter a good buck.

When you find a fresh track worthy of your attention, resist the temptation to follow it exactly. To do so, you would have to keep your eyes on the ground and might miss seeing the deer when you catch up with it. Also, deer watch their backtracks. They are very aware that they may be being followed, and their senses are alert to anything that might be coming along behind them.

HOW TO FOLLOW TRACKS

Instead of dogging a track, hunt parallel to it. Follow the track just long enough to get a good idea of the direction in which the deer is traveling. Then swing off about 100 yards on the downwind side of the track and move in a parallel direction. Move slowly, stopping often to study your surroundings. If you fear the deer has changed direction, you can move back upwind until you strike the track again and can reassess its direction.

Just before a buck beds down, he usually turns downwind so he can get the scent of anything following his track, and he moves to an area of slightly elevated ground that offers cover and a view of his backtrack. By traveling parallel to his track 100 yards or so to the downwind side, you are moving in a position that is likely to take you straight to where the buck has bedded. Keep your eyes peeled.

If the buck's track crosses in front of you, headed downwind, freeze. Assume the buck is moving to a bedding site nearby, and search closely for it. Scrutinize every piece of heavy cover and every elevated position.

TRACKS GOING DOWNWIND LEAD TO BEDS

Whenever tracks lead you to believe the buck is moving toward its bed, you are in a perfect position to use a grunt call or rattling antlers to bring the buck from his bed to you. (See Chapters 12 and 13 on calls and rattling.)

If you don't see him, back up 100 yards on your own track, then begin paralleling his track again as it leads downwind. If the buck senses your pursuit and evades you, backtrack him to his bedding site, and remember that spot as a place to check another day when you can come in from the downwind side.

Wherever deer tracks lead you, you will be learning more about the behavior patterns of the deer in your area. Following a fresh track may lead you to a buck, but more often it will be the accumulated knowledge you gain by studying where older tracks go that will put you in position for a shot.

How Weather Affects Whitetails

ALTHOUGH THE WEATHER can have a great effect on whitetail behavior, it affects hunter behavior even more. Remember, deer have to stay out there, regardless of the weather. They never leave their haunts. It is the hunters who make excuses and don't appear when the weather turns nasty.

Strong winds, torrential rains, and heavy snowfalls all drive deer into protective cover. They bed down in places where an overhead canopy of vegetation breaks the wind and blocks the precipitation to some degree. As long as a storm lasts, deer generally remain bedded in one place.

During bad storms it seems as if there are no deer in the woods. They all seem to disappear. The deer trails show no fresh tracks, and you will not see a deer moving unless you or some other hunter jumps it from its bed.

KNOW WHERE DEER BED

Hunting during bad storms can be notably miserable and disappointing *unless* you know where deer are most likely to hide out. If you know where they are bedded, you have a good chance of jumping deer up close. The lashing wind, wet leaves, or deepening snow will permit you to move through the woods without making disturbing noises. Strong winds also break up your scent and make it more difficult for deer to know where your scent is coming from until you are close. If you have a good idea where deer are bedded during stormy conditions, you have a chance to sneak into that area unobserved and peek around. Sometimes you will be able to spot deer in their beds before they see you. Most often, however, you will be unaware that deer are nearby until one suddenly leaps up very close to you.

If it has seen you, the deer will come up running. But if it has just caught your scent and has not yet seen you, the deer may just stand up in alarm. If you see it rise up before it sees you, you have a good chance for a standing shot at close range.

My hunting partner Jim Henry shot a dandy 8-pointer with a massive 24-inch rack that dressed out over 220 pounds one stormy day in Maine. It had blown and rained hard for two days, and there were no hunters in the woods. Everyone was waiting for the storm to pass.

Bored with hanging out in camp, Jim decided to go out anyway. He pulled on a foul-weather suit, left the tent, and went uphill under the cover of a high canopy of white pine. Eventually, he came to a thick patch of short pines with interlapping branches. He had not gone far into the thick stuff when his eyes caught movement and a blur of brown as the enormous buck rose from its bed and took a step into the open at very close range. Jim's rifle was at his shoulder with the crosshairs settled behind the big buck's shoulder before it saw him and had a chance to flee.

After a Storm

On the day after a storm, deer become very active as they move to feed. At such times, your best bet may be to take a stand in an area where you know deer were feeding before the storm and wait for them to come to you.

Extremely cold weather also causes deer to bed down and wait. Usually they seek shelter from wind in spots that are open to the warming rays of the sun. When deep snow and extreme cold combine, look for deer on southwest-facing slopes that offer the best exposure to sunshine.

On the day after a storm, deer become very active as they move to feed following their period of inactivity.

When moonlight is bright on clear nights, deer remain active later and may, therefore, be less active during daytime, particularly if hunting pressure is heavy. Whenever lots of hunters are in the woods during the day, deer quickly become nocturnal and do more of their

Though bucks rarely feed during the rut, they move from one active feeding area to the next in search of does in breeding condition.

feeding and breeding under the cover of darkness, remaining hidden during more of the day.

ACTIVE PERIODS

In regions where deer are not overly harassed by hunters and are following their natural patterns, they are commonly active during a great part of the day. Deer must accumulate fat during autumn to sustain them through winter, so they feed heavily during daylight hours unless they are afraid. Deer actually spend more time feeding than doing anything else.

Groups of deer commonly move from bedding areas to feeding places just before dawn, usually traveling on well-established trails and walking in single file, often led by an older doe. Once in their feeding area, they separate and move individually, taking a few bites here, then moving on to take a few more bites somewhere else. They rarely stay in one place long enough to consume the food source entirely.

Deer commonly continue to feed until mid-morning, when they bed down close to their feeding area if not disturbed. They get up and feed again briefly at midday, bed down through the early afternoon, and move out to feed again just before sundown.

Although mature bucks do little feeding during the active breeding season, they travel from one active feeding location to the next in search of does in breeding condition. When bad weather causes does to seek shelter and stop feeding, the bucks bed down, too, since it is harder for them to find does that are inactive and not leaving scent or signs. A mature buck that has joined up with a doe before a storm begins may remain with her until the storm passes.

Deer can sense bad weather coming and are very active in the last few hours before a storm begins. They feed heavily and then move, often long distances, to sheltered places where they wait out the storm.

EFFECT OF WIND

Low wind velocities have little effect on whitetail behavior, but as velocities increase, deer seek shelter. Studies indicate that the reaction of deer to high wind is similar, regardless of whether the deer are forest dwellers or farmland feeders. When the wind is strong, deer are less active.

Because wind noise covers the sounds you make walking, windy days can be very productive hunting days, allowing the hunter more opportunities to get close to deer that are hidden in sheltered places.

Soft Rain, Light Snow

When soft rain or light snow is falling, deer remain active, moving normally from feeding to bedding areas. Such days are great hunting days because the damp forest floor allows you to move very quietly, and the precipitation reduces the deer's visibility and makes your movement less noticeable.

Hunters become more noticeable on bright sunny days, however. Gun barrels flash in the sun, catching the attention of deer at great distances. Not only are hunters easier to see, but their shadows precede them, causing flashes of dark and light to fall on tree trunks, which deer are quick to perceive. On sunny days a careful hunter tries to move in the shadows, avoiding open sunlight as much as possible.

Most Difficult: Popcorn Days

Crisp, cold days when the forest floor is covered with frozen leaves that sound like popcorn when you walk on them are the most difficult days for hunters. Deer can hear your approach from long distances and will move away before you ever see them. On such days your best bet is to move quickly to a good stand and wait for deer to come to you. You can hear them coming for a long way, too.

I shot one of my biggest bucks on a popcorn day in New Hampshire. The woods were so noisy that every step caused a commotion no matter how carefully I placed my feet. Finally, I just gave up trying to be quiet and clattered my way uphill to a favorite observation spot. I pushed the leaves away with my feet, settled down against a comfortable tree trunk, and remained still.

Every time a squirrel moved, I jumped. A mouse in the leaves sounded like a moose. All of the forest sounds were incredibly loud. The noisy conditions did not stop the bucks from patrolling, however. I heard this one coming when he was still several hundred yards away. He was up on the ridge above me, and when he started to come down it sounded as though he was crashing through thin ice.

I had plenty of time to turn toward him and get my gun ready. His antlers came into view first, and they were impressive, glinting in the low winter sunlight. He was trotting through open hardwoods, sounding like a freight train, and came past me at a range of 40 yards. He never knew I was there until I fired.

How to Dress
for Deer Hunting

I F YOU'RE COLD, you won't be able to sit long on a deer stand. If your clothes are bulky, you won't be able to walk comfortably through the woods. And if your clothes make noise, you won't be able to move with the stealth that successful deer hunting requires. So when you dress for deer hunting, keep these three objectives in mind: warmth, comfort, and quietness.

Once, two friends who had not done much serious deer hunting joined my group on a trip to Maine. They brought the most amazing collection of clothing I had ever seen, including entire suits for different days and different weather conditions. A look in their tent revealed arctic windproof snow pants that were so bulky they couldn't walk in them, huge orange jackets rated to -20° F, enormous stuffed hats, down-filled mittens, electric socks, and great big Mickey Mouse boots that caught on everything they tried to step over.

Well, Maine can be cold in deer season, and you have to prepare for snow and ice and cold rain, but these outfits were ludicrous. Not only were they too bulky to allow comfortable movement, the outfits were so well insulated that my friends would sweat if they tried to walk any distance. And worst of all, the clothes made noise.

I was sitting quietly on a ridge one snowy morning when I heard unusual noises sounds, sort of yipping sounds, below me, coming my way. My first thought was that there were coyote pups nearby, chasing each other through the woods.

But it wasn't coyotes, it was my friends. Rather, it was my friends' clothes. The outer shells of their insulated suits were made of nylon, and as they moved through the underbrush, branches whipped and zipped against them, creating the yipping sounds I had heard from a couple of hundred yards away. No way would they ever get close to deer in those outfits.

One deerless week in those outfits convinced my friends that their clothing choices had been disastrous. When they returned the following year, they dressed like the rest of us, in layers of soft clothing that can be added or taken off as the weather dictates.

When you dress for deer hunting, keep these three objectives in mind: warmth, comfort, and quiet. Dress in layers of soft, loose clothing.

WHAT TO WEAR

I have settled on the following clothing as my regular deer hunting outfit.

- *Next to the skin:* polypropylene long underwear, sock liners, and glove liners. "Polypro," as it is often called, wicks moisture from your skin so that sweat does not build up when you exert yourself.
- *Second layer:* Thick wool/polypro-blend socks. Insulated rubber boots. Light or heavy wool pants, depending on the weather. Wool or fleece shirt. Thin wool or fleece gloves. Wool cap with earflaps.
- *Top layer:* Loose-fitting wool or fleece jacket. Wool or fleece is warm, light, and quiet. It doesn't rustle or snap against brush.
- *Extras:* In a fanny pack or day pack, carry a down or polyester vest that you can put on under your outer layer when you stop to sit for a long period. Take the vest off and carry it separately when exerting yourself. A lightweight waterproof rainsuit can be rolled up and stuffed in your pack on inclement days.

For an extended hunt, you will need two such complete outfits so that one is always dry. Sock liners can be rinsed out each day and dried quickly with heat. Take one new pair of heavy socks for each day you expect to be away.

The Rut: Buck Behavior and How to Take Advantage of It

MATURE BUCKS rarely travel with does and antlerless deer except during the rut, or active breeding period. The rut can begin as early as September and continue through January, though peak breeding activity occurs in November in most northern states and later farther south.

As the rut approaches, bucks that have been traveling together in tolerant small groups throughout the summer and early autumn become aggressive and begin fighting to establish dominance. The largest, heaviest bucks have the advantage and usually emerge as the winners of pushing contests they enter into with smaller bucks. When bucks of relatively equal size and strength confront each other, however, the pushing contests can become violent and sometimes escalate into mortal combat.

Although fights to the death do occur, they are rare. Sometimes two heavily antlered bucks jam their racks together with such force that they cannot be separated, and the bucks starve to death locked in their fatal embrace. More commonly, big bucks inflict damaging wounds on one another, striking each other with their hooves, raking each other's shoulders and ribs, and puncturing each other's ears, necks, and bodies with their antlers.

It is rare to see bucks in battle, but the signs of their struggles are commonly found as the rut begins. The ground will be torn by hooves over a room-sized space, and tufts of hair will be found on the forest floor and stuck on underbrush. Often one buck will force the other into a blowdown that limits his maneuvering room and prevents him from turning to deflect the other's antlers.

Sometimes these royal battles occur in the presence of a doe, but usually dominance is settled before the breeding season gets into full swing. By the time does are entering estrus, most bucks are avoiding contact with other bucks of equal size, although they often continue to tolerate the company of inferior bucks or large subdominant bucks that do not challenge their claim to breeding rights.

WITNESSING A BATTLE

I once witnessed a battle between two equal-sized 8-pointers that were pushing and shoving each other around in an open stand of hardwoods one November day when the rut was well advanced. A doe was standing nearby, feeding but paying little attention as the two bucks clashed antlers, pawed the ground, and glowered at one another.

Suddenly a little fork-horned buck appeared on the scene. At first he eyed the battle from a distance. When he determined that the big bucks were fixated on one another, however, the little buck trotted in, nuzzled the doe, then mounted and bred her not 20 yards from where the bucks were fighting. When they finished, the little buck and the doe disappeared together without the fighting bucks ever noticing them.

ANTLER RUBS

The sparring begins as soon as bucks lose their antler velvet in early autumn. Once this takes place, you begin to see bright marks on saplings along deer trails where bucks have rubbed their antlers. The size of a rubbed sapling sometimes indicates the size of the buck that rubbed it. Bigger bucks tend to rub on trees of larger diameter. When you see a rub on a tree 3 inches or more in diameter, you are in the home range of a large, mature buck.

The size of saplings rubbed by bucks while polishing their antlers can tell you something about the size of the buck that did the rubbing. Bigger bucks rub bigger saplings.

THE ESTRUS PERIOD

The active breeding period begins when does begin entering estrus, or breeding condition. Individual does come into estrus at different times, but the condition lasts only about 24 hours. If the doe is not bred during her first estrus period, she will come into estrus for 24 hours once again 28 days later.

During the first month of the active breeding season, dominant bucks search constantly for does that are entering estrus. When a buck finds a doe in breeding condition, he will usually stay with her for about 24 hours and may copulate with her several times during that period. While they are together the buck goes wherever the doe leads, and he will usually fight or drive off any other buck that threatens to come close to her. As her estrus period passes, the doe becomes unwilling to accept the buck and leaves him. The buck then strides out across his range, searching for another doe that is ready to breed. Dominant bucks frequently breed more than a dozen does in a season.

Bucks Get Less Wary

As breeding season progresses and more and more does have conceived and avoid contact with bucks, fewer does enter breeding condition. The bucks now have to search even more diligently to find those that remain.

Consequently, as the rut continues the buck barely eats or rests. He loses weight rapidly and becomes gaunt. His entire purpose is to find does in breeding condition. In his exhausted, sex-crazed state, he becomes less cautious, less wary. Now he is using every sense to locate does, and he becomes particularly susceptible to scents and sounds indicating a doe in estrus is nearby. (See Chapters 11–13 on using scents, calls, and rattling antlers to attract bucks during the rut.)

Bucks seek does by checking feeding areas. They travel routes that cross well-established deer trails, searching for the scent of does in breeding condition. When a buck catches the scent of a doe in estrus, he follows her trail with neck extended and head close to the ground, sniffing the doe's tracks and places where she paused to urinate. The buck occasionally curls his upper lips for a few seconds, savoring the doe's scent, and may utter a guttural grunt from time to time.

Scrapes

In areas most frequented by does, bucks make numerous ground scrapes to advertise their availability. They paw back the leaves and

Scrapes are made by bucks that are in breeding condition. They are usually made beneath a hanging branch, which the buck licks and brushes with scent from the glands in his forehead. Bucks return to refresh scrapes regularly during the rut.

bare the earth in a space beneath a low overhanging branch. They lick the overhanging branch and rub it with their forehead glands and antlers, leaving scent. Then they urinate on the tarsal glands inside their rear knees to leave scent in the pawed space. As they leave, they stamp their footprint clearly in the center of the scrape.

Bucks return to these scrapes regularly during the breeding period to refresh them and to check for signs that does have visited the scrape and urinated near it, indicating a willingness to breed. Much of the scraping activity occurs at night in areas where hunting pressure is heavy. Nevertheless, any place where numerous scrapes are found close to one another is an excellent place to encounter a buck.

During the peak of the rut, bucks are also seized by the inclination to thrash bushes and saplings with their antlers in mock battles. These antler-torn shrubs and saplings are found along well-used deer trails, indicating a mature buck passes there regularly. The thrashed vegetation is one more sign by which a buck communicates his presence and availability. Scent from his forehead glands clings to the battered bushes, advertising his desire to breed.

DOMINANT BUCKS DIE EARLY

The rut leaves mature bucks thin and exhausted. With winter close upon them and food scarce at the end of breeding season, there is little time to regain fat before the rigors of winter begin to take their toll. If subsequent temperatures are severe and the snow gets too deep to paw back and expose food, mature, dominant bucks often succumb. Consequently, large, dominant bucks often have shorter lifespans than subdominant bucks that enter winter fatter and less stressed from fighting and breeding.

Hunting in Groups

DRIVES HAVE BEEN an effective means of harvesting deer since long before gunpowder was invented. Native Americans used fire to drive deer and other game to waiting hunters armed with spears or bows and arrows. Some tribes built elaborate fences to funnel driven animals to waiting hunters and then sent lines of people with noisemaking devices through the woods to flush the game.

Today, deer drives usually consist of a line of noisemaking hunters moving through the woods toward other hunters waiting quietly at stands along escape routes deer are expected to take. Some states now consider large-scale deer drives unsafe, unsporting, and inconsiderate of other hunters and limit the number of individuals allowed to participate in group hunts. In regions where deer live in very thick cover that is difficult to hunt by other methods, however, large-scale deer drives are still sometimes the method of choice.

Deer are not always susceptible to being driven. Those that have survived drives may have become very savvy and may refuse to run ahead of the drivers. Instead, they seek hiding places, lie down, and hope the drivers will pass by without seeing them.

HUNTING IN SMALL GROUPS

Most states allow small groups of hunters to assist one another, even where organized large-scale drives are banned.

The most effective way for a small group of hunters to help one

The most effective way for small groups of hunters to help one another is to use individual still-hunting techniques within a small area. If one hunter jumps a buck but does not have a good shot, the deer may move into the range of another hunter.

another is to use individual still-hunting techniques within a given area. The hunters choose a defined section of a deer range and then designate a specific route for each group member. Rather than attempting to drive deer and steer them to waiting hunters, they separate widely and then progress through the woods in an agreed direction.

Each person operates as a still-hunter, but knows the other hunters are only a few hundred yards on either side. The hope is that if one hunter jumps a buck but doesn't have a good shot, the deer will move within range of another hunter in the group. When a deer is down, hunters who work together know they will have help getting the carcass out of the woods.

The trade-off in this kind of hunting is that several hunters moving in the same direction in close proximity can't help but create noise and motion that may alert deer and cause them to flee before anyone gets within close range. A single hunter, moving stealthily, might come closer to the deer being spotted.

There is no denying that a certain sense of camaraderie attends hunting in small groups. It's nice to know that your hunting partners are not far away and to share some of the memories of the hunt, and there are times when small groups can flush deer to one another that would be impossible for a single hunter.

FANNING OUT ON A TRACK

If good tracking conditions exist, an effective method is for one hunter to follow a track while the others fan out a few hundred yards on either side of the track and still-hunt in whatever direction the track leads. When the track moves into thick, protective cover, the outside hunters swing forward in a pincer movement that may encircle any bedded buck and flush him out past one of the other hunters. If the buck tries to escape on his backtrack, he will run into the hunter who has been following the track.

HUNTING IN PAIRS

Two hunters working together can be particularly advantageous. One follows the track while the other moves parallel on the upwind side. If the tracker jumps the deer and does not get a shot, there is a chance the deer will escape into the wind and pass within close range of the upwind hunter.

USING HAND-HELD RADIOS

Group hunting is most effective if the members carry hand-held radios and stay in regular communication. Modern, battery-operated pocket-sized radios are available at affordable prices that are perfect for this kind of hunting.

Using hand-held radios enables hunters to keep track of one another's location and to call for help when assistance in needed.

My hunting partners and I usually head off in separate directions from our starting place and hunt alone, but we turn on our radios and swap information every hour on the hour, and we may change our hunting plans depending on what is reported. If one of us is seeing lots of deer signs in a certain type of habitat and the others are not finding signs in different habitats, we learn where to go.

Radios enable us to keep track of one another's position on the topographic maps we always carry. If one of us gets a shot, we immediately report to the others what happened and whether or not we need assistance. Of course, if one of us gets into any difficulty, we can call the others for help.

During radio checks we keep the volume very low and speak in whispers or low tones so the deer don't hear us. To save batteries and eliminate the chance of having a radio squawk unexpectedly when a deer is close, we keep the radios turned off except at agreed-upon radio check times.

If one of us thinks a deer is close and does not want to turn on the radio, that hunter skips the radio check but is expected to come on the air and check in 30 minutes later.

Hunting from Stands

IN AREAS where hunting pressure is heavy and lots of hunters are moving through the woods, it is often best to hunt from a stand. Other hunters will keep deer moving, and your chances of seeing a deer from a stand overlooking the junction of heavily traveled trails are good. Likewise, in areas where hunter activity is slight and deer are moving on their habitual routes from bedding areas to feeding places, your knowledge of their habits will help you locate a stand in a good place to intercept them. The stand can be in a tree or on the ground. The more important consideration is not its height but its location.

WHERE TO LOCATE YOUR STAND

The best way to determine where to locate your stand is to do lots of preseason scouting. It is also important to remember from one year to the next where deer moved during previous autumns. Check tracks, droppings, antler rubs, and ground scrapes to discover where deer habitually travel on the routes from bedding areas to feeding areas, and locate your stand overlooking a place that shows the most deer activity.

LEARN AUTUMN FOOD SOURCES

Bear in mind that feeding locations change as deer adjust their diets from summer food to foods that become available in autumn. Deer that feed on lush green vegetation in summer may switch to acorns and beechnuts in the fall, so scout out where the heaviest concentrations of those mast food sources are located, and choose stand locations accordingly.

If you hunt deer in farm country, locate your stand overlooking a trail that leads to a crop the deer will be feeding on in late autumn. Some of the crop fields deer use in summer will have been harvested or plowed under by fall and so will be of no further use to deer. You want your stand to overlook trails that lead to cornfields, alfalfa fields, or green winter wheat fields that still offer desirable food in late autumn.

HAVE MORE THAN ONE STAND

Don't have just one stand. If you hunt the same territory year after year, you will gradually accumulate more knowledge about where deer move according to changing food sources, weather, and hunting pressure. As you determine the places deer use frequently under various circumstances, look around for good spots that overlook these areas and offer cover and clear shots in several directions.

When you find these choice locations, spend some time and build a comfortable stand that you can return to when conditions indicate deer may be using that area.

TREE STANDS

Tree stands are commonly favored by bow hunters because they must make a physical movement—drawing their bows—before they can shoot. This eye-catching movement can alert nearby animals, so the bow hunter puts the stand high in a tree above the vision of most deer.

Firearm hunters gain the same advantage when they make their stands in trees. Deer are less likely to see them, and the hunter's scent is somewhat dissipated before it drifts to ground level.

A wide variety of comfortable, strong tree stands that provide a solid seat for a hunter perched in a tree are available in sporting goods stores and through catalogs. Tree-climbing models, which enable the hunter to shinny up and down trees, can be mounted in a

Deer are less likely to see hunters in tree stands because they do not expect danger from above and are not in the habit of looking up.

tree with little difficulty and can be moved from one place to another quickly and easily.

BUILDING YOUR OWN

Personally, I prefer to build tree stands out of wood and leave them in place permanently. Rather than just having a seat perched in a tree, I am more comfortable on a larger wooden deck with a comfortable seat surrounded by a low railing.

Look for a clump of trees with trunks at least 8 inches thick 20 feet above the ground overlooking an established deer-feeding area or a junction of well-used trails. Then seek permission from the landowner to construct a deer stand there. On the site, build a ladder that reaches a place at least 20 feet above the ground. Next, construct a frame of 2 × 4s spiked to the tree trunks, deck the 2 × 4 frame with 1½-inch thick boards, and make a comfortable seat in the center. Erect a railing of lumber or strong branches 3 feet above the deck and cover it with camouflage material that will stop the wind and hide you from view. Now hang branches from the railing to break up the outline of the stand. As a last step, tie a rope from the railing that reaches to the ground so you can pull your unloaded rifle up into the stand at the beginning of your hunt or lower it to the ground when you are ready to leave.

STANDS AT GROUND LEVEL

As much as I enjoy the view from a tree stand, I must admit that I am an impatient hunter and find it difficult to sit in one place for a long period if I am not seeing anything. Consequently, a great deal of my hunting is done from stands that I rough together on the ground.

The stands are nothing fancy—usually just some loosely arranged branches piled around a tree trunk to break up my outline and a comfortable place to sit that allows me to turn and face in different directions. The location of these stands is based on wind direction and where I expect a buck to come from.

I have a number of these favorite stands at various locations in the few square miles of woods that I hunt most often. When I am hunting new country I make one of these rough stands whenever I find a place that fits my criteria. (It must overlook an area or junction of trails that shows heavy deer use and offer a clear shot in several directions.)

As I move through the woods hunting, I am constantly aware of my proximity to these chosen stopping places, and I move from one to another, settling into each one with the intention of staying until I am prompted to move on.

PAY ATTENTION TO AIR MOVEMENT

Before choosing a stand, check the wind direction. Then choose a stand that will be on the downwind side of the trails or feeding area you will be overlooking so that your scent will not be carried to the places from which you expect the deer to come. Even if there is no real wind, general air current patterns will affect the direction in which your scent will travel. In the morning, on windless days, air currents move uphill as the air temperature rises. This indicates that you should take a stand on the uphill side of the trails or feeding areas on windless mornings and expect deer to be moving in from below or from the sides.

Air currents are reversed in the late afternoon, flowing downhill as the air temperature drops on windless days. Thus, you should take a stand on the downhill side of the trails or feeding area on windless evenings and expect deer to come from uphill or from the sides where your scent will not be carried.

MY FAVORITE STAND

My favorite stand is a 20-minute walk from my hunting camp. That is where I head before dawn every morning and where I wind up for the last hour of daylight most evenings.

It is on an edge of a rise in the ground, overlooking a wide hardwood bench where deer feed regularly and a junction of trails that deer use to travel up and down the valley. Above the stand is another rise of ground overgrown with heavy brush where deer commonly go to bed down during daylight. Thus, I can expect deer to be moving both above me and below me and can face in either direction according to the direction of the air currents.

The stand itself is just a wooden seat built within the angle of the broad crotch of an ancient maple that fell to the ground many years ago. I can sit in that crotch and oversee a wide swath of country. The embracing arms of the fallen tree hide my body so only my head protrudes, and I have a solid rest for my rifle no matter which direction I face.

I have killed several good bucks from that stand over the years. It pays off just often enough to keep me going back.

I had an uncle whose favorite deer stand was a tall, hollow stump that overlooked a junction of trails in a large wood lot that stood between two enormous cornfields in a big river valley. He used a chainsaw to cut the stump down to chest height and built steps up the back side of the stump so he could climb in. As a seat inside the stump, used a 5-gallon bucket with a boat cushion on top of it.

He could sit comfortably inside that stump all day, and he often did. He was protected from wind and could move around without being seen. When a deer came along he could turn in any direction to face it.

He killed a good buck from that stump every year I can remember until he grew too old to hunt and turned the stump over to a younger member of his hunting group, who still takes good bucks there regularly.

10

What Is Still-Hunting, and How Do You Do It?

THE TERM "still-hunting" is misleading because a good still-hunter does not stand still but moves. But the still-hunter moves so slowly and so unnoticeably that you rarely see any motion.

You see a still-hunter in the shadows, leaning against a tree. A few moments later you see the hunter stopped beside another tree a few feet farther on, but you have to watch carefully to actually see the movement.

Still-hunting works anytime, but it is particularly effective when deer are not moving because of storm conditions or when hunting pressure has made them seek shelter. "You can stay on a good stand all day and not see a thing if the deer aren't moving," notes expert New Hampshire still-hunter Alfred Balch. "If the deer don't move and the hunter doesn't move, there's not goin' to be an encounter."

A good still-hunter relies on the ability to get within close range of a deer by using stealth and knowledge of deer behavior. The hunter expects to see deer before being seen and, consequently, moves in a state of suspended animation.

WIND DIRECTION

Still-hunters stay alert to wind direction and adjust their hunting course so they will be moving into the wind (with the breeze in their faces) or across the wind (with the breeze on their cheeks). If the wind is on their backs, their scent will be blown ahead of them, warning deer of their approach.

You can't move too slowly when you are still-hunting. If you are seeing deer tails bouncing away, you are moving too fast. Those are deer that saw you before you saw them.

Deer have extremely keen noses and can pick up the scent of a hunter at very long distances. When they smell a person approaching, they're gone.

You Can't Move Too Slowly

You can't move too slowly when you're still-hunting. If you see deer tails bouncing away, you're moving too fast. Those are deer that saw you before you saw them. If you have to look down at the ground to place your feet when you move forward, you're walking too fast. Good still-hunters look at the ground and plan their next few steps before they leave a stopping place. Then they move forward a few steps with their eyes up, watching their surroundings for any changes while they are in motion.

Move in the shadows, and avoid bright spots. When you stop, stop on the shaded side of a tree or other large object.

MOVE IN THE SHADOWS

Effective still-hunters move in the shadows, avoiding bright, open places. When they stop, they stop on the shaded side of a tree or other obstruction that will break up their outlines. At each stop they pause for a long time, searching the surrounding woods until they are satisfied that no deer is watching them. Their eyes are alert for anything that doesn't quite fit with its surroundings—anything that might be a piece of a deer that is partially hidden. Then they check the ground, planning their next few steps, before they move again. They move with utmost stealth.

HOW TO WALK QUIETLY

In order to move quietly, the still-hunter places the feet carefully with each step, keeping weight on the back foot while the front foot moves ahead. The hunter avoids branches that might catch the advancing foot and sets the foot down heel first. When the heel is secure, the still-hunter rolls forward slowly onto the front foot, crushing the twigs beneath the foot into the ground rather than breaking them and causing them to snap loudly.

The little crushing sounds your feet make at ground level don't carry far, but sounds made above ground level echo through the woods with loud reports that deer notice from long distances. Knowing this, the still-hunter is careful to avoid catching a foot on upright branches, thumping a boot on a log, or tipping over loose rocks and making them clunk. The hunter avoids low branches that could snag clothing and snap.

DON'T BUMP SAPLINGS

When passing through groves of saplings, still-hunters avoid bumping the slender trunks, which would cause the upper branches to thrash and rattle, alerting nearby deer to their approach.

KNOW WHERE DEER WANT TO BE

Advancing cautiously through the woods in this manner, still-hunters use their knowledge of deer behavior to steer their progress. They know from experience where deer are most likely to seek shelter, and they approach those places with extreme caution. They use the terrain, the shadows, tree trunks, boulders, and blowdowns to their advantage, always trying to make themselves unnoticeable.

STILL-HUNTING TECHNIQUES ARE ESSENTIAL

Using the still-hunting techniques described above will make you a more effective deer hunter in any situation. Most still-hunters combine still-hunting with hunting from stands. They use still-hunting techniques as they move to a stand, and then they settle in to wait and watch during periods when they expect deer to be moving on their own. When deer don't seem to be moving, still-hunters slowly move into an area where they expect to find bedded deer.

11
CHAPTER

When to Use Scents

THE USE of scents to attract deer is not new. In Paleolithic times, native hunters wrapped themselves in gamy-smelling skins and anointed themselves with scents made from animal extracts that were either attractive to game or served to mask human odors

In recent years a huge industry has grown around the manufacturing of attractive deer scents and human scent eradicators, so today's hunters have a vast array of deer-hunting scents available to them.

There is no question that scents can be helpful when used properly. But be warned: The use of too much scent can be worse than no scent at all, and there is no scent that can be relied on to attract deer when careful hunting techniques are ignored.

HOW SCENTS WORK

Bucks in the rut are on constant alert to find does in breeding condition. They are constantly searching for the scent of does that are entering estrus.

Does in estrus mark trails and ground scrapes with their urine to signal bucks that they are in breeding condition. The urine of does in estrus, therefore, is a particularly powerful attractant during the rut.

Modern manufacturers collect and bottle urine from does raised in zoos and on farms that produce venison for the market. Then they use glandular extracts as well as urine actually collected from does in estrus to produce scents and lures advertised as being sexually attractive to bucks in the rut. Read the labels carefully and check with other hunters to find out which brands seem to work best.

How to Use Scents and Lures

Although some loud-smelling hunters apparently believe otherwise, it is not necessary to soak your clothes in doe urine to be an effective deer hunter. Instead, hunters can carry doe-in-estrus urine in a small bottle with either a spray cap or a cap that emits droplets. As they proceed through the woods to their stands, they stop occasionally to scatter a few drops or emit a small mist of spray at random spots. Some hunters attach scent-saturated pads to their boots in order to leave a trail of attractive scent.

When you come to an area that shows heavy signs of buck use in the form of ground scrapes, antler rubs, and tracks, squirt some doe-in-estrus urine into the ground scrapes and then pin a scented ball of cotton head high above the ground nearby. Then take a stand that overlooks the scrape from the downwind side.

Food Scents

Sexually attractive scents are most effective once the rut begins. Bucks, however, feed heavily prior to the rut and at that time may also be attracted to the scent of particularly appealing foods. Most popular is apple concentrate or a molasses-based scent applied in a feeding area upwind from a deer stand.

The use of actual apples or molasses would be equally effective, but using real foods to bait deer is prohibited in most states during hunting season.

Cover Scents

Cover scents are used to mask human odor. Most popular are skunk essence and the oils of pine, fir, and cedar, all of which emit lasting natural forest odors that may help overcome human scent. An artificial skunk cover scent recently came on the market that does not emit the noxious odor until two separate scentless ingredients are mixed, thus avoiding the problem of the powerful skunk scent leaking or spilling on clothing.

To use cover scents, put a few drops on cotton balls and pin them up around the location of your deer stand so that the scent travels out away from the stand with air currents from any direction.

Users must be careful to avoid applying too much cover scent. Heavy doses smell unnatural and may actually alarm deer.

SCENT-ERADICATING SOAPS

Scent-eradicating soaps, said to remove human odors from clothing and skin, are also available from a number of manufacturers. The makers recommend that deer-hunting clothes be washed in these soaps before the hunt and that hunters wash their hands and face with the soaps before going into the woods.

Many hunters who believe that tobacco, cooking odors, and wood smoke permeate clothing and make them more noticeable to deer hang their hunting coats and pants outside to dry rather than near the stove. Some hunters stuff cloth bags of pine or balsam needles in their clothes at night to gather a natural scent.

Used sparingly, scents, lures, cover scents, and soaps may help to attract deer and to eliminate or overcome human and other alarming scents. But scents and lures are unlikely to attract a deer to a place it does not want to be, and cover scents never make you totally unnoticeable to deer. No matter what scents or lures you use, you will be a more effective hunter if you put yourself in places where the signs indicate deer want to be and use air currents to your advantage by making sure your scent is not being blown into the area where you expect the deer to be.

Deer Calls
and How to Use Them

DEER are generally quiet creatures, but they do vocalize at certain times.

Anyone who has been around deer much recognizes the snort or "blow" that an alarmed deer emits to warn other deer of danger. Snorts are often repeated again and again as deer bound away from perceived dangers, and they may be heard from immobile deer that have spotted movement or heard a noise that warns them of something they have not yet identified. Snorts are more often made by antlerless deer than by mature bucks, which usually do not vocalize alarm but take evasive action silently.

Less often heard are the communications between does and fawns. Does sometimes use a low grunt to call their fawns when ready to offer a nursing opportunity, and fawns sometimes bleat to call their mothers when they're afraid or lonesome.

From the hunter's standpoint, the most important deer vocalizations are the loud grunts bucks commonly make when trailing does during the rut and the grunt-snort combination bucks sometimes make when confronting one another and threatening to do battle. Both calls can be used to attract bucks during the rut.

Many hunters learn to make loud and effective grunt calls and snorts with their mouths, using no manufactured calls whatsoever. Those who have mastered these calls have the advantages of being able to call instantly, without having to dig around in their pockets for a manufactured call at moments when a buck is seen passing in the distance, and to vary the call and the volume according to the situation.

Historically, not many hunters have been able to master voice-calling. Museums contain many examples of hand-held deer calls that were crafted by native hunters long before the manufacturing industry got into the act. Today, sporting goods stores and hunting catalogs are crammed with deer calls that can work well when used by practiced callers.

HOW TO USE THE GRUNT CALL

When a buck in the rut is following the trail of a doe, he often emits long, drawn-out grunts that can be compared to the sounds made by a rusty barn-door hinge. The call is commonly repeated two or three times over a period of about a minute.

The sound is attractive to other bucks because it suggests that there is a buck nearby trailing a doe in breeding condition. A buck that hears the sound may move in its direction, hoping to get on the doe's trail himself, even if it means he will have to drive the grunting buck off the trail.

If you are the "grunting buck," you're likely to get a shot. Bucks that respond to grunt calls are often large, mature, dominant bucks that are not afraid to rush into a situation that may result in a fight.

A grunt calls sends the signal that a buck is trailing a doe in breeding condition. When they hear that sound, other bucks may be drawn in its direction, hoping to get on the doe's trail themselves.

Grunt calls work best during the rut when it is not too windy and sounds travel farthest. Use the grunt call from your stand or whenever you see a distant deer passing that is not coming toward you. Make two or three long, drawn-out calls over the space of about a minute. Then stay silent for about 20 minutes before you repeat the series of two or three calls.

SUCCESS CAN HAPPEN FAST

I know an outfitter in Maine who built deer stands in excellent places, but his clients' success rate was low because the clients would get cold or lonesome and wander back to camp rather than stay on their stands. "I needed a way to make them stay in the woods," he recalls.

The outfitter bought a box of grunt calls off the shelf. The next season he presented a call to every client and told them, "blow it two or three times every 20 minutes and don't move—the bucks'll run right over you."

He was as surprised as the hunters when three clients bagged big bucks the first morning. Each one said the bucks just came running shortly after they had blown the calls. The next day a couple more big bucks were bagged by hunters who followed the outfitter's advice.

"When the word spread that the calls worked, everybody in camp started believing in them. That year our success rate soared, and it has stayed high ever since. To tell you the truth, I don't know if the difference is because the hunters are using calls or because they now have a reason to stay on their stands rather than wandering back to camp. Either way, using the calls sure helped us," he reports.

Stories abound regarding deer over-running hunters who use grunt calls. Hunters who have seen a buck come running after they have used a call are ardent believers in the call's effectiveness. The calls do not guarantee success, however. Most hunters who use grunt calls have never seen a buck come to them.

GRUNT-SNORT COMBINATIONS

The grunt-snort combination is made by bucks that are squaring off to fight. It is an excellent call to make in combination with antler rattling. (See Chapter 13 on rattling antlers.)

BLEAT CALLS

Hunters commonly use calls that imitate the bleat of a fawn during antlerless seasons to attract mature does to their stands. The bleat is given softly two or three times every 20 minutes from a stand or by a moving hunter who thinks a deer may be nearby.

During the rut the bleat call can sometimes attract a doe being followed by a buck. It can, therefore, be an effective way to bring in a preoccupied buck not likely to be attracted to a grunt call, scents, or rattling antlers.

KNOCKING ON WOOD

When a buck wants to call in nearby does, he sometimes does so by knocking his hoof repeatedly against the root of a tree where it enters the ground. The resonant knocking sound can be heard for a fair distance.

Once, when I was hunting in Quebec, we inadvertently jumped a bunch of deer that bounded off, snorting and flagging their tails in alarm. "Get down," whispered my French-Canadian guide. He knelt at the base of a big fir tree and unsheathed his hunting knife. Then he knocked the handle of the knife loudly five times against the root of the tree, just where it entered the frozen ground. Five minutes later he repeated the sounds; about 5 minutes after that, he repeated them again.

Then he raised his head above the undergrowth to peek. Suddenly he dropped down and motioned for me to get ready. He gestured that the deer were returning and put his spread fingers up by his head to indicate that one was a buck. A minute later four antlerless deer came into view, heads up, ears fanned, tails flicking in anticipation as they searched for the maker of the sounds. Then came the fifth deer. I could see his antlers before I could see his body. A moment later he stepped into view—a fine 8-pointer that dressed out just under 200 pounds.

CHAPTER

Rattling Antlers for Big Bucks

J UST AS ABORIGINAL HUNTERS used scents and calls to attract deer, they also rattled antlers together to create the sounds of two bucks fighting as a means of luring bucks into bow-and-arrow range.

During the rut, bucks are attracted to the sounds of other bucks fighting because they expect the fight to be over a doe in estrus. Big bucks in particular can't resist checking out the sounds of a fight, hoping to drive off the combatants and take the doe they are fighting over for themselves.

Rattling is effective during three stages of the rut. Just before does begin coming into estrus and active breeding begins, bucks do a lot of fighting to settle dominance issues. When they hear the sounds of two bucks fighting, other bucks are drawn to the sounds. When a fight begins bucks run to watch, just as people do. During the peak of breeding season, the sounds of a fight indicate that the bucks are battling over a doe in estrus. After the peak of breeding activity passes, dominant bucks continue to search for does that have not yet conceived. Now the competition between bucks becomes even more intense. They respond to any sound or scent that indicates a doe in estrus may be near. I have had bucks respond to rattling antlers from late October through early January in the northern states and provinces where I hunt most frequently.

Some hunters believe that the size of the antlers used for rattling has a bearing on the size of the bucks that respond. They say that both medium-sized and large bucks are drawn to the sounds of medium-sized antlers clashing together, but that only large bucks are attracted to the sounds made by large antlers.

62

The sounds of a buck fight, made by rattling antlers, indicates that two bucks are fighting over a doe that is in breeding condition. Other bucks may be drawn to the sounds, hoping to claim the doe themselves.

That has not been my experience, however, I have used the same pair of relatively heavy antlers that I took from a large 8-point buck many years ago and have seen bucks of all sizes drawn to the sounds they make. I think *how* you use them is more important than how large the antlers are.

HOW TO USE RATTLING ANTLERS

To rattle antlers most effectively you should try to simulate as closely as possible the sounds of two bucks really fighting. Picture a buck fight in your mind as you clash, twist, and rattle your antlers in ways that make the sounds of the fight that you are mentally creating. Stamp your feet, crack brush, grunt, and snort. Make it a dramatic performance.

Start with light antler sounds, which can be heard by bucks that may be nearby. As you continue, increase the volume and the intensity

Clash the antlers together, then twist them back and forth under pressure. When you reach the end of a rattling sequence, continue to twist the antlers together as you pull them apart.

of the fighting sounds in order to be heard farther away. Make each rattling session last about 30 seconds, then put down your antlers, pick up your rifle, and watch for an approaching deer. If no buck appears after 3 minutes, repeat the rattling session for another 30 seconds, then put down the antlers and pick up your rifle once more. Continue to repeat 30 seconds of rattling and 3 minutes of rest until 15 minutes have passed. If a buck has not shown himself after 15 minutes, the chances are good that one will not appear. Then it's time to move to another spot.

HOW BUCK FIGHTS SOUND

When bucks fight, they begin by lightly sparring with their antler tips. This activity usually escalates into pushing and twisting contests that includes light antler sounds, followed by the thumping of hooves and the sounds of grinding antlers. The bucks continue pushing and twisting for a few seconds at a time, followed by periods of rest.

If pushing and twisting fail to prove which buck dominates, the action increases. Now the bucks clash their antlers together with greater force, then twist and shove, making heavier, grinding antler sounds as each buck attempts to get past the other's antlers and injure his opponent.

Hooves thump repeatedly as the two attempt to throw each other off balance. Sometimes one buck is thrown to the ground with a loud body slam. The bucks push each other into blown-down timber, causing cracking and crashing sounds. At pauses in the battle, they may emit loud grunt-snort combinations and stamp their hooves or paw the ground furiously as they work up their rage for the next clash of antlers.

Try to make all of these sounds. You can make hoof thumps by hitting the butt of an antler on the ground. Pawing sounds can be made by raking the tips of an antler on the ground forcefully. Smash some dry brush with your feet to imitate the sounds of bucks fighting amid underbrush and blown-down timber. Add grunt-snort calls, particularly during rest periods.

The most effective antler-rattling sounds are made by clashing the antlers together, then twisting them back and forth under pressure, just as bucks do. When you reach the end of each rattling session, continue to twist the antlers together forcefully as you pull them apart. This action adds a very realistic sound because bucks usually stop fighting when the eye of one is threatened by the antler tip of the other, and he backs away as the other buck continues to push and twist, thus pulling the antlers apart under force.

As long as you have a little underbrush around you, don't be afraid of having your movements seen by a buck drawn to the sounds. He expects to see the movement of two bucks fighting and will not usually be put off by the sight of your partially screened actions. In fact, he may be attracted by seeing a little movement. He is more likely to become wary if he does not see some movement coming from the source of such violent sounds.

WHERE TO RATTLE

Good locations for rattling sessions have these requirements: They are located in country that indicates lots of buck use; they offer some cover, so you are not right out in the open; they offer visibility, so you can see and shoot in all directions; and there are dry branches around for you to crack and smash as part of your fighting-sounds repertoire.

If you are following a buck track that crosses an opening and then leads into heavy cover, don't expose yourself by crossing the opening. Instead, crouch down in a semicovered location and put on a dramatic rattling performance. If the buck is in the thick cover, he is likely to come out to your sounds, and you will have a clear shot as he approaches through the opening.

Likewise, whenever signs indicate that you are in a heavy-use deer area, rattling may be effective in bringing a buck to you that you might not otherwise see. If you are hunting big country, mixing still-hunting and rattling can be very effective. Pause and rattle whenever you come to a good place. If nothing responds after 15 minutes or so, move on slowly to the next good location and rattle again.

If you are hunting from a stand, put on a 15-minute rattling session about once an hour. You may be heard by a buck that is traveling through the area, out of your range of vision.

When conditions are right, rattling antlers may attract bucks at any hour of the day. I have actually had more bucks come to rattling antlers between 11 A.M. and 1 P.M. than at any other times. Whenever the wind is still and the woods are quiet, rattling may work.

THE SECRET IS BEING HEARD

Rattling works only if it is heard. Unless you are in country with a high deer population, your rattling will *not* be heard by deer more times than it *is* heard. Don't expect frequent success.

Once, when hunting in an area that bragged 35 deer per square mile and a 50 to 50 buck to doe ratio, I rattled up three bucks in one day. That's the best I've ever done, and that was in an area in which I was probably being heard by a buck every time I put on a rattling performance.

WHY BUCKS SOMETIMES REFUSE TO RESPOND

To be effective, your rattling must not only be heard, it must be heard by a buck that is willing to respond.

Bucks that are traveling with does will usually not respond to rattling. They already have what they want, so why risk losing it by entering into a fight? In areas where hunting pressure is high, bucks that have been scared by seeing people in the woods are less apt to respond. If they have been duped before by a hunter rattling antlers, they may avoid the sounds. Rattling works only when hunting pressure is limited and where bucks feel safe and are following their sexual instincts, not running and hiding. Subdominant bucks that have already lost a few fights may remember their previous whippings and want to avoid further indignities. Old bucks may have passed breeding age and no longer respond to any sexual attractants. On top of all that, you have to be close enough to a responsive buck for your sounds to be heard.

Does respond to rattling almost as often as bucks do when conditions are right. If you see a doe approaching, don't be quick to move away. Does that respond to the sounds of a buck fight are often traveling with a buck. He may follow the doe toward the rattling sounds even though he may not be responsive to the sounds of a fight himself.

HOW BUCKS APPROACH

I usually expect almost immediate action if rattling is going to work. Most of the time I see the buck within the first 5 minutes after

When they respond to rattling, bucks keep hidden in cover as they approach. Suddenly, they just appear, staring straight at you.

I begin a rattling session. I may continue for 15 minutes without seeing one, but I know that most of the time, if I have been heard by a responsive buck, I'll see him right away.

Usually what you see does not look like a buck coming toward you. You'll see a slight deer-like movement in the distance, or a deer tail will flash far up ahead. Sometimes you'll see the whole deer, but he may appear to be moving away. The rule is this: If you see any deer movement when you are rattling, keep it up. You've been heard. Give the buck a chance to respond.

Some bucks come in as if they were being pulled on a rope. Others bound into view and run right up to you. Usually the approach is much less dramatic. You'll see an ear and the curl of an antler sticking out from behind a tree. You'll wonder how the buck got there without you having seen him before. The deer will keep trees and obstructions between you as he approaches, and you won't see him most of the time. Keep your rifle near at hand.

The buck will probably travel toward you on a course that will take him past you on one side or the other as he attempts to get downwind of your position. If he succeeds in reaching your downwind side, he will pick up your scent and drift off, so be prepared to shoot before he gets downwind.

Once in a while a buck will just appear right in front of you. His neck will be fully extended, his ears will be flared, his nose will be searching for your scent, and his eyes will be focused on the spot where you are making the sounds. Either way, when a buck comes to your rattling antlers, it will be one of the high points of your deer-hunting career, and you will become a confirmed believer in rattling antlers.

How to Make Rattling Antlers

Plastic rattling antlers are available, and some people make antler sounds by using hard wooden rods, but real antlers make the most realistic sounds. Antlers sawn off freshly killed deer make the best sounds, but shed antlers that you find in the woods can also be used if they are still hard.

Antlers of medium thickness are choice. They should have three long tines and a curve that makes them comfortable to handle. If they have a short brow tine near the base, cut it off and file the base of the tine flat so it will not stab you in the hand when you are performing a violent rattling scene. Use a wood file to smooth the shafts of the antlers into comfortable hand grips. Drill holes in the butts of the antlers so you can connect the antlers with a short line if you wish. To keep the antlers resonant, coat them with linseed oil at the end of each hunting season and hang them up. Next season, wipe off any excess oil.

Cut off the short brow tine and file the antler shafts smooth to make a comfortable hand grip. Give the antlers an annual coat of linseed oil to keep them resonant.

Use of Map and Compass

ALWAYS CARRY a topographic contour map of any big-woods tract in which you plan to hunt. Before you begin your hunt, study the map to learn the geographical features of the country you will be entering. Memorize the major landmarks, noting where roads, railroads, rivers, and streams lie and the directions they follow. Note the relationship of the highest hills or mountains and the locations of lakes, swamps, cliffs, and gorges that may block your way.

Studying a topographic map before you enter a piece of country lets you form a mental picture of the land, which will help you keep track of where you are in relation to your starting point once you begin hunting.

MAP SCALE

Be sure to check the scale of your map to determine how much distance one inch equals. The scale will be printed on the edge of any good map. The distance per inch will either be stated in words or be represented on a small bar graph.

For hunting purposes, the most widely used maps are the 1:24,000- and 1:62,500-scale topographic maps issued and sold by the U.S. Geological Survey. On maps drawn at a scale of 1:24,000, one inch equals 2,000 feet. On maps drawn at a scale of 1:62,500, one inch equals about a mile.

These maps are available for all local regions from sporting goods, outfitting, and backpacking equipment stores or can be ordered directly from the U.S. Geological Survey, Information Services, Box

Study a topographic map of your hunting area before you enter a piece of country, and become familiar with the major landmarks. Note obstacles that may block your way.

25286, Denver, CO 80225; phone 1-800-USA-MAPS. For those with Internet capability, *www.recreation.gov* or *www.blm.gov* are two excellent sites that provide information on sources of topographic maps and public lands that are open to hunting.

USE MAP AND COMPASS REGULARLY

Basic map and compass use is very simple. If you get in the habit of using your map and compass regularly whenever you are in the woods, keeping track of where you are and noting how to get back to your starting point becomes almost second nature. However, if you don't refer to your map or compass until you have already lost your bearings, they may be of little assistance.

WHAT KIND OF COMPASS DO YOU NEED?

For basic hunting use, you don't need an elaborate compass. A simple ball compass that pins onto your hunting jacket or a hand-held compass with clear markings for North, East, South, and West with half-stops in between will give you all the information you need to keep rough track of your bearings. Precision instruments that can be adjusted for declination and are capable of measuring in half degrees are intended for more sophisticated use than most deer hunting.

A COMPASS ONLY POINTS NORTH

Regardless of how simple or how sophisticated your compass, remember that all compasses do only one thing: They point to Magnetic North. Period. That's it. No compass tells you the way home unless you already know where home is in relation to Magnetic North.

That's why you need to use your compass together with a good large-scale contour map that shows the relationship of landmarks that you will be able to see from certain vantage points. (If you know that a certain lake is *west* of your starting point, for example, you can calculate when you see the lake lying *south* of your current position that the general direction from the lake back to your starting point is *southeast.*)

Warning: Always hold your compass some distance away from metal objects such as your rifle, knife, belt buckle, and so on. Because the compass needle is magnetic, nearby metal objects will cause the needle to skew away from Magnetic North.

STARTING OUT

Before going into the woods, find and mark your exact location on your map. Note where major landmarks are in relation to your starting place and in relation to the area you plan to hunt. (If I go in here, this road where I parked the truck will be on my east, this mountain I plan to hunt will be north of me, this stream will be on my west flowing south, and so on. My general way back to the road from that country is east.)

KEEP TRACK OF TIME

Wear a watch and note the time you entered the woods. As you progress, refer to your compass regularly in order to keep track of the directions you are traveling in and the time you spent moving in each direction. Whenever you knowingly change direction, make a mental note of your turn so that you can remember your route later. Check your progress on the map at regular intervals. (I went north for an hour to the edge of this swamp, then I hit a deer track that was headed west. I followed it along this side hill for about 45 minutes and then moved straight uphill to the north for half an hour. Tracing that route on the map with your finger will give you a pretty good idea of where you are. Now look at your starting point in relation to your current position.)

Once you get into the habit of keeping track of where you are in relation to your starting point, you will always know the general direction that will take you back. Noting the time you took traveling in each direction lets you predict how long it will take to retrace your route if you decide to do so.

FOLLOWING A COMPASS COURSE

To follow a compass course in an intended direction, hold the compass in front of you at waist level and turn your body until the direction you wish to follow is at the top (12 o'clock) of your compass dial. You are now facing in the direction in which you want to go.

Now, look as far out in that direction as you can see and pick a landmark that you will be able to keep in view as you walk toward it. In thick, overgrown country you may have to pick a prominent tree, boulder, ledge, or other nearby object that you can clearly identify. In open country, you may be able to choose a more distant feature, such as a mountaintop or lake, as your reference point.

Once you have chosen a physical feature in your intended direction of travel, walk toward it until you either reach it or it disappears from view. When that reference point is of no further value to you, hold your compass in front of you again and once more turn your body until your intended direction of travel is at the top of the compass dial. Now choose another landmark in your intended direction and move toward it until you either attain it or it disappears from view. Continue to repeat this procedure and you will stay on a straight line traveling in your intended direction.

To follow a compass course, hold your compass in front of you, then turn your body until the direction you want to follow is at the top of your compass dial. Pick a distant landmark in that direction, then walk to it. Keep repeating this procedure. Check your progress on the map at regular intervals; by doing this you will always know the general direction back to your starting point.

Don't Doubt Your Compass

Trust your compass. No matter where you think north is, your compass knows better. The only time to doubt your compass is if the needle refuses to settle in one direction while you are standing still, or if the needle is stuck and refuses to move as you turn the compass.

Once, while hunting in the Iron Range of Minnesota, I was in an area so rich in iron ore that my compass needle turned constantly. Unable to use the compass, I kept my bearings by staying close to running water that I knew led back to the river where we were camped.

Global Positioning Systems

Hand-held global positioning systems (GPSs) are now available at prices from less than $100 up. If the batteries are fresh, you have an open view of the sky, and the unit is dry and in first-rate condition, a hand-held GPS can determine your location within 50 yards or less, can record the course you followed, and can show you the most direct route back to your starting place or any other location you have marked.

But don't rely on a GPS entirely. Units sometimes fail or are unable to contact the satellites that send the information. The GPS may also suggest that you follow a route that is blocked by impassable features such as lakes, cliffs, swamps, or other phyical configurations it cannot recognize.

The best reason I know to carry a GPS while hunting is to be able to report your exact position by radio if you need help. With or without a GPS, don't go into the woods without a map and compass and an understanding of how to use them.

Firearms and Cartridge Choices

THE CHOICE of a deer rifle is entirely personal. Any rifle or caliber that is legal in the states in which you plan to hunt is capable of killing deer cleanly when aimed accurately at a target that is within its killing range.

In the brushy, timbered country where whitetails spend most of their daylight hours, the need to make a shot beyond 200 yards is rare; most whitetails are shot at ranges of less than 100 yards. However, there are occasions when long-range, open shots present themselves, and you may find yourself needing a rifle capable of long-range accuracy and extended killing range.

CHOOSING AN ACTION

You must first choose the type of action that suits you best.

Lever-action rifles can be less expensive than other types and are light and fast handling. They are the choice of many hunters who believe them to be more convenient for carrying in thick cover. Most popular in 30/30, .300 Savage, and .35 Remington calibers, and usually considered to be "100-yard rifles," they usually lack long-range accuracy and "knockdown power." Another disadvantage is that lever-action rifles must be unloaded by jacking cartridges through the chamber with the hammer cocked. This requirement presents a safety concern that does not exist with bolt-action, pump, and semi-automatic rifles, which are loaded and unloaded through a separate magazine rather than through the chamber.

Pump-action and semiautomatic rifles are fastest to use and may be operated without taking the rifle from the shoulder. Their devotees want a gun that offers the quickest follow-up shots. Pumps and semiautos come in a wide variety of high-speed calibers that offer relatively flat trajectory and extended killing range.

Bolt-action rifles are slower to operate, but they can seat a cartridge in the chamber tighter, which can result in superior long-range accuracy. Bolt-action rifles are offered in the widest choice of calibers and are the most popular type of action overall.

"BRUSH BUSTERS"

A persistent myth is that big, slow bullets "bust brush" without losing accuracy and that bullets traveling at higher speeds are deflected when they hit twigs. Don't be misled. The truth is that all bullets are deflected when they hit brush, and the deflection becomes more severe as range increases.

Ideally, you want to be able to deliver your bullet on target by shooting through holes in the timber where no interference will be encountered. In order to do that, you'll need a rifle that allows you to get your sights on your target quickly and a cartridge that will deliver a bullet to your target before it gets past such an opening.

"FLAT-SHOOTING" CALIBERS

There is no such thing as a "flat-shooting" rifle, caliber, or bullet. All bullets from all rifles drop at the same rate from the instant they leave the barrel. The difference is that faster-traveling bullets cover more distance in a given time than do slower bullets. Therefore, in the time it takes for all bullets to drop an inch, the faster bullets will have gone farther than the slower bullets. Thus, a bullet that covers 200 yards in the time it takes all bullets to drop an inch is termed "flatter-shooting" than a bullet that travels only 100 yards in the time it takes all bullets to drop an inch.

BULLET TRAJECTORIES

The table on page 79 gives a comparison of the trajectories of bullets in the 11 most popular deer-rifle calibers. As you can see, the faster

It takes more than 800 pounds of energy per square inch for a bullet to achieve the shocking power and penetration necessary to consistently kill deer under most circumstances. The maximum distance at which a bullet maintains 800 pounds of energy per square inch should be considered the deer-killing range of that cartridge.

the bullet travels, the less it drops at normal deer-hunting distances. Slower bullets drop farther at the same distances.

Most hunters agree that the best calibers for general-purpose big-game hunting in North America fire 150-grain bullets at speeds in excess of 2,000 feet per second at 200 yards range and drop less than 8 inches at 300 yards.

"KNOCKDOWN POWER"

It takes more than 800 pounds of energy per square inch for a bullet to achieve the degree of shocking power and penetration necessary to kill a deer under most circumstances. The maximum distance at which a bullet maintains 800 pounds of energy per square inch should, therefore, be considered the deer-killing range of that cartridge. To be on the safe side, you really ought to shoot a deer rifle that delivers 1,000 pounds of energy per square inch to your target at whatever range is required.

The table on page 79 compares the "knockdown power" of the

same list of popular cartridges in terms of the number of pounds of energy per square inch they deliver downrange.

You can see from the tables that bullets from .250 Savage-, Winchester 30/30-, Winchester .32 Special-, and Remington .35-caliber rifles drop fast and push the limits of knockdown power when the range reaches 200 yards, whereas the other cartridges drop less and still carry plenty of knockdown power all the way out to 300 yards and beyond.

Trajectory Table

Cartridge	Bullet Weight	Velocity 100 yds.	Velocity 200 yds.	Drops 100 yds.	Drops 200 yds.	Drops 300 yds.
.243 Win.	100	2,790	2,540	0.5	2.2	4.7
.250 Sav.	100	2,410	2,070	0.6	3.0	6.4
.257 Rob.	100	2,540	2,210	0.6	2.7	7.7
.264 Win. Mag	100	3,260	2,880	0.4	1.6	4.2
.270 Win.	150	2,400	2,040	0.7	3.0	7.8
.280 Rem.	150	2,580	2,360	0.6	2.6	6.5
30/30 Win.	150	2,020	1,700	0.9	4.2	11.0
30–06 Spr.	150	2,670	2,400	0.6	2.4	6.1
.300 Sav.	150	2,390	2,130	0.7	3.0	7.6
.308 Win.	150	2,570	2,300	0.6	2.6	6.5
.32 Win. Sp.	170	1,870	1,560	1.0	4.8	13.0
.35 Rem.	150	1,960	1,580	0.9	4.6	13.0

Energy Table

Cartridge	Bullet Weight	Energy at 100 yds.	Energy at 200 yds.	Energy at 300 yds.
.243 Win.	100	1,730	1,430	1,190
.250 Sav.	100	1,290	950	695
.264 Win. Mag.	100	2,360	1,840	1,440
.270 Win.	150	1,920	1,380	1,020
.280 Rem.	150	2,220	1,850	1,510
30/30 Win.	150	1,360	960	680
30–06 Spr.	150	2,370	1,920	1,510
.300 Sav.	150	1,900	1,510	1,190
.308 Win.	150	2,200	1,760	1,400
.32 Win. Sp.	170	1,320	920	665
.35 Rem.	150	1,280	835	545

Rifle Sights

YOU HAVE A CHOICE of open, peep, or telescopic sights.

Open sights are at their best when you are shooting at a running target at close range in heavy cover because you can keep both eyes open and see your target as well as your surroundings as you aim. This enables you to anticipate when a running target is going to come into an opening and give you a clear shot.

Open sights, however, are very limiting when you want to take a shot at longer range. At 100 yards a deer looks so small that a broad front sight covers its entire chest when you are using an open sight. At longer ranges, open sights don't really tell you just exactly where you are aiming on the deer because they block out so much. Furthermore, people with "older eyes"—who have difficulty focusing on the sight and the target at the same time—find open sights give them a blurry sight picture, even at close range.

Open sights are fast to aim, but you must remember to get your face down tight on the gunstock and to pull the front bead all the way down into the bottom of the rear sight notch or you will shoot high or to the side no matter how well you have sighted-in the rifle.

Better open sights can be adjusted up, down, and sideways by use of a slide-and-locking screw arrangement. Less-expensive open sights must be driven to make sideways adjustments, and their elevation adjustments can be crude and may require filing.

Open

Open sights are fast to aim but block the view of your target at longer ranges.

Peep sights are very accurate because your eye automatically puts any object you focus on in the center of the space in which you see it.

Peep

PEEP SIGHTS

A peep sight is a small hole in a disk through which you view both your target and your front sight. The disk is mounted on an adjustable base attached to the rifle's receiver. Click-stop adjusting screws permit the shooter to move the disk up, down, and sideways for precise sighting-in.

Peep sights work because your eye automatically puts any object you focus on in the center of the space in which you see it. Your eye will automatically place your target in the center of the peep hole and line it up with the front sight. Once you have adjusted the sights to line up at the exact spot where your rifle delivers its bullets, you can expect to shoot very accurately with a peep sight.

The disadvantages of a peep sight are that the aperture hole sometimes gets clogged with snow or debris, and, like the open sight, the front bead may cover so much of the target at longer distances that it becomes difficult to know exactly where you are aiming.

TELESCOPIC SIGHTS

That leaves us with telescopic sights as the best answer for most hunters, most of the time.

No other sight gives you the ability to be as precise in your bullet placement. Furthermore, once you have adjusted the crosshairs to center on the exact point to which your rifle delivers its bullets at a certain range, you can be sure that at that range every bullet will go to the spot where the crosshairs cross, regardless of how you hold your head or the rifle itself.

Telescopic sights give you almost surgical precision when it comes to bullet placement. A telescopic sight magnifies the target according to its power, allowing you to center the crosshairs exactly where you want the bullet to strike. They also magnify light, as well as objects, making such sights extra helpful in dim light.

As magnification power increases, however, the width of the field of view you can see through the scope decreases. Too much power reduces the field of view to an unacceptable degree and may make your viewing picture too narrow for you to keep a running buck in view as he bounds in and out of cover.

For that reason, most manufacturers recommend no more than a 2½-power scope on rifles intended for use at short range and a 4-power scope for guns expected to be used on targets out to 200 yards.

VARIABLE SCOPES

The ideal scope, in my view, is the variable scope. A variable scope has a ring-type dial that you turn to increase or decrease the magnification. Changing the magnification does not affect the range at which the scope has been sighted-in. My personal favorite is the Leupold 2½-to-8× variable scope (× = power). I have one on every big-game rifle I own.

I carry my scope set on $2^1/_2×$ when I'm walking in order to have the widest possible sight picture should I jump a deer up close. When I stop to watch or wait on a stand, I adjust the scope to 4× so I can magnify my target when I see a deer approaching. Just before I shoot I can adjust the scope to an even higher power, which gives me a large picture of the deer and allows me to place the bullet exactly where I want it to go.

Up–down adjustment

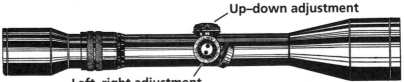

Left–right adjustment

Telescopic sights give you almost surgical precision when it comes to bullet placement. A telescopic sight magnifies your target according to its power, allowing you to center the crosshairs exactly where you want the bullet to strike.

When I have a walking or standing target, I often screw the scope all the way up to 8× when I'm ready to shoot. This gives me the ability to place my bullet precisely and make a killing shot without damaging any more meat than necessary.

CHOICE OF RETICLES

When you buy a telescopic sight, you have a choice of reticles, which give different sight pictures depending on your requirements. A heavy post-and-crosshair reticle is quick to get on target and easier than others to see in dim light, but it may be too coarse for fine bullet placement at longer ranges. Thick crosshairs are also helpful in dim light, but may block out part of your target at long range. Thin crosshairs allow the most refinement in bullet placement, but may be difficult to see in dim light.

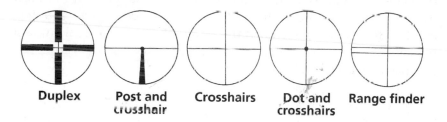

| Duplex | Post and crosshair | Crosshairs | Dot and crosshairs | Range finder |

The reticle I like best is called a duplex. It has dual-thickness crosshairs, which are medium thick in the outer segments so I can get on my target in a hurry. The center segments of the crosshairs are of very thin wire, which allows me to refine my bullet placement.

Telescopic lenses vary in price according to how well they are made and the quality of the glass. Buy the best scope you can afford.

Sighting-in Your Rifle

SIGHTING-IN MEANS adjusting your rifle's sights so they line up at exactly the point where your rifle delivers its bullets at whatever distance you choose. Remember, you are not changing the point at which the bullets strike; you are changing the point at which the sights line up. Your rifle will deliver its bullets on the same trajectory regardless of how the sights are adjusted. When you have adjusted the sights to line up at the point where your rifle delivers its bullets at your desired range, your rifle is sighted-in, or "zeroed," for that particular distance.

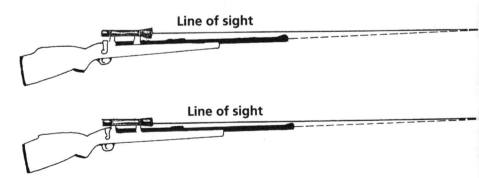

All bullets begin to drop as soon as they leave the muzzle. In order to compensate for the drop, we tip the barrel up slightly and then adjust the sights to line up at the spot when the bullet will drop to our target elevation.

BULLETS DO NOT RISE

Bullets begin to drop the instant they leave the muzzle. Despite what you may have heard, bullets do not rise for a while and then begin to drop. They just drop.

To make the sights line up at the point a dropping bullet will impact at a range of 200 yards, we have to tip the rifle barrel up at an angle slightly above our actual line of sight to compensate for the drop that will occur as the bullet travels 200 yards. When you look at a diagram showing the bullet traveling above the line of sight, you could get the impression that the bullet rises after it leaves the muzzle. It doesn't. We have merely fired the bullet at a slightly upward angle, and that angle keeps the constantly falling bullet above our line of sight as it travels to its target.

SIGHT-HEIGHT FACTOR

The height at which the sight is mounted above the bore is another factor. The bullet actually begins its flight from below our line of sight because the sights are mounted considerably above the bore of the rifle. Thus, when we fire a bullet from a barrel that has been tipped up to compensate for bullet drop, the bullet coming from below our straight-to-the-target line of sight will cross that line at two places.

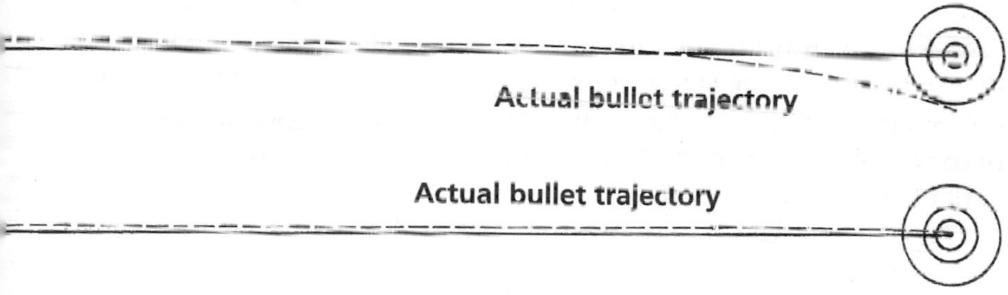

Actual bullet trajectory

Actual bullet trajectory

The upward-fired bullet will first intersect our line of sight a short distance beyond the muzzle. It remains above our line of sight throughout its downward-curving trajectory and eventually drops to intersect our line of sight again.

Sight-in at Short Range

Using trajectory tables published by ammunition manufacturers, we can accurately predict how high above our line of sight a bullet must be at 50 yards in order for it to drop back to our line of sight at any target distance. This gives us the ability to do our actual sight-in shooting at a convenient short range even though we actually want our bullets to drop to our line of sight and be on target at much longer ranges.

From the table on page 88, you can see that a .280 Remington 150-grain bullet that hits 0.6 inches above the line of sight at 50 yards will be 0.9 inches above the line of sight at 100 yards, right on target at 150 yards and 2.3 inches below the line of sight at 200 yards. Knowing this, I need only sight-in my .280 so that its bullets hit 0.6 inches high at 50 yards and I know that it is sighted-in (zeroed) for 150 yards. If I need to make a 200-yard shot, I know that I must aim a little more than 2-inches high.

Mounting the Scope

A telescopic sight should be mounted so that you see a full sight picture when you bring the rifle to your shoulder. Using a screwdriver that perfectly fits the screw slots, loosen the mounting rings and slide the scope forward or back to increase or decrease the distance between the scope and your eye until you find the point at which all dark obscurity vanishes and you see the full sight picture.

Next, while the mounting rings are still loose, twist the scope tube in the mount until the crosshairs are perfectly vertical and horizontal. Once these adjustments are made, the scope will be adjusted to suit the manner in which you hold your rifle. Tighten the mounting screws again.

Now, mount the rifle to your shoulder and aim at the sky. Are the crosshairs sharp and black, or do they appear somewhat fuzzy? If they are fuzzy, you need to focus the eyepiece. The eyepiece is focused by loosening the eyepiece lock ring, then turning the eyepiece clockwise or counterclockwise until the crosshairs are sharp and black. When the adjustment is made to your satisfaction, tighten the eyepiece lock ring and you're ready to start sighting-in.

SIGHTING-IN PROCEDURE

1. Before shooting your rifle, clean it well to remove any dirt or grease that may be in the bore, and check that the sight mounts are very tight.
2. Always sight-in using the same cartridges you will use for hunting. Sighting-in is not the time to get rid of odd lots of cartridges.
3. Set up a target either 25 or 50 yards from the muzzle. (A bullet from a high-powered rifle drops so little between those initial distances that for deer-hunting purposes you are unlikely to notice any difference in long-range accuracy, and a target at 25 yards is more convenient to use.)
4. Use a bench rest with a sandbag or a log with a folded blanket or coat for support. Rest your hand on the support, not on the rifle barrel; then rest the rifle on your hand. Never rest the rifle barrel on a hard surface because the recoil will cause the barrel to jump, spoiling your shot.
5. Aiming at the center of the bull's-eye each time, fire three shots. This should give you a close group that shows where the bullets are hitting.
6. Measuring from the center of the group, determine how many inches high or low and how many inches to the right or left the bullets are hitting from the center of the bull's-eye.
7. Adjust the sights to compensate for the difference.

Telescopic and receiver/peep sights have click-stop adjustment screws that usually move the sight picture by one-quarter minute of angle per click. A minute of angle (four clicks) equals one inch at 100 yards.

Adjust the sight in the direction you want the bullets to go. If the bullets are hitting to the right of your point of aim, adjust the sight to the left. If you are hitting high, adjust toward low.

If you are using a receiver/peep sight, adjust in the same manner.

If you are using open sights, move the rear sight in the direction you want the bullet to go. However, if you need to adjust the front sight, move it in the opposite direction. If your open sights do not have windage adjustments, they must be driven right or left with a hammer and a brass or wooden drift pin. Rear-sight elevation is usually adjusted up or down by moving a graduated steel insert beneath the sight tang. The front sight can be filed down if it is too high.

9. Adjust the point of aim until your bullets are grouping where you want them. Remember that you are sighting-in at short range, so use the bullet path table to determine how high above your point of aim bullets must impact at 25 or 50 yards in order to be right on target at the longer range you want to be "zeroed" at.

10. Once you have the rifle shooting the correct degree high at 25 or 50 yards, go out and shoot it at your designated zero range of 100, 150, or 200 yards and make any necessary final sight adjustments.

**Bullet path above or below line of sight (inches)
on rifles with low-mounted scopes or metallic sights**

CARTRIDGE	WEIGHT	50 YDS.	100 YDS.	150 YDS.	200 YDS.
.243 Win.	100 gr.	+0.5	+0.9	Zero	−2.2
.250 Sav.	100 gr.	+0.2	Zero	−1.6	−4.7
.257 Rob.	100 gr.	+0.1	Zero	−1.3	−4.0
.264 Win. Mag.	140 gr.	+0.5	+0.8	Zero	−2.0
.270 Win.	150 gr.	+0.6	1.0	Zero	−2.4
.280 Rem.	150 gr.	+0.6	+0.9	Zero	−2.3
.30/30 Win.	150 gr.	+0.5	Zero	−2.6	−7.7
.300 Sav.	150 gr.	+0.3	Zero	−1.8	−5.4
.308 Win.	150 gr.	+0.2	Zero	−1.6	−4.8
.30–06 Win.	150 gr.	+0.6	+0.9	Zero	−2.2
.32 Win. Sp.	170 gr.	+0.6	Zero	−3.1	−9.2
.35 Rem.	200 gr.	+0.8	Zero	−3.8	−11.3

18

Picking Your Target: Where to Shoot a Deer

I HAVE NO RESPECT for hunters who want to knock a deer down any way they can. My goal (and I hope yours, too) is always a one-shot kill. Ideally, I want a clear shot at a walking or standing deer. I want to be able to place my bullet precisely, so that even if the deer runs off, I know that it will fall dead within a short distance.

This is not to say that you should never shoot at a running deer. I have killed a number of deer that were moving fast, but they were at close range when I fired, I had a clear view of my target, and I was able to place the bullet where I wanted it. When given an opportunity to take a chance shot at a deer that I don't have "dead to rights," I always pass up the shot and wait for a better opportunity. I want to kill the deer, not wound it, and I don't want to ruin any more meat than necessary.

I believe the ideal way to kill a deer is to shoot it through the lungs. A lung-shot deer often runs off a short distance, but it nearly always drops dead within 100 yards or so. During the time it takes the animal to run that 100 yards, its heart continues to pump blood from its body tissues into the destroyed lung area, which bleeds out the carcass efficiently and makes the flesh much better tasting.

WHERE TO AIM

If the deer is passing broadside to me, my target is the "engine room" right behind the shoulder, halfway between the top and bottom of the deer's body. It's a big area that contains the deer's most vital organs. If my bullet flies true, it will destroy the lungs. If it hits a bit high, it will strike the spine with instant paralyzing effect. If my aim is low, the bullet will hit the heart, just below the lungs. To the rear of the lungs is the liver. A liver shot will also cause an immediate bleed out and quick death.

If a deer is coming toward me, my target is the center of the chest, just where the neck joins. A bullet striking there will destroy lungs and liver. If a bit high it will strike the neck vertebrae; if low, it gets the heart.

When a deer approaches at an angle that does not offer a straight-on or perfect broadside shot, the "engine room" may be blocked by a shoulder. When this is the best shot I can get, I aim directly at the point of the shoulder. This shot will sacrifice about two pounds of stew meat, but the bullet will pass through the shoulder directly into the vital area.

If the deer is moving away from me, I try for an angle shot behind the ribs into the "engine room." If that is not possible, I aim just above the shoulders at the base of the neck. If the shot is a little high, it will hit higher on the neck, which is also deadly. If the bullet hits low, it will hit the spine and paralyze the deer.

Neck and spine shots do not produce the beneficial bleed out that a lung shot provides, but they are deadly and usually drop the deer in its tracks. A heart shot is also deadly, of course, but it also fails to cause a complete bleed out since it destroys the pump that pulls the blood from the tissues when an animal's lungs are destroyed. Also, the heart is a small target; if your aim is low, you will shoot under the deer.

SPEED MEANS LEAD

If a deer is moving fast but offers a clear shot at the vital area, you can hit your mark only if you compensate for the deer's speed and lead your target, just as you must when shooting a shotgun at flying game.

When you shoot a high-powered rifle at a running deer at a range of 100 yards or less, you must fire when your sights are some distance ahead of the shoulder, depending on the range and the animal's speed. When shooting a slower cartridge, the lead must be even greater.

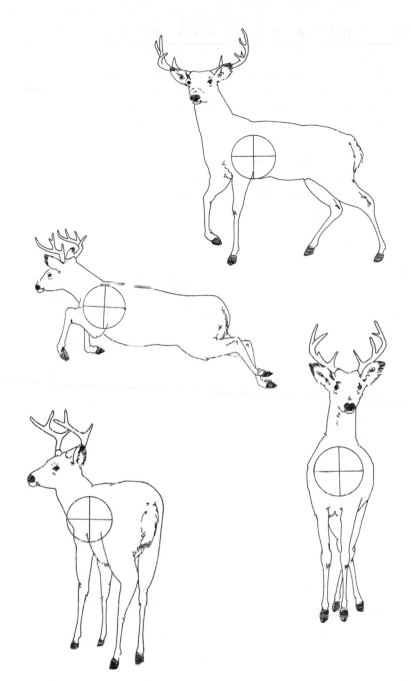

From any angle, your target should be the heart-lung area. For a broadside shot, aim just behind the front shoulder, halfway between the top and bottom of the deer's body. From head-on, aim at the base of the neck in the center of the chest. If the deer is angling away, aim just behind the ribs. If it is running straight away from you, aim above the back at the base of the neck.

The table below explains why so many hunters miss running deer. How accurately can you place a bullet fired at a running deer when leads such as this are required? These figures are for a 30/30 rifle shooting a 170-grain bullet at a deer moving at typical slow-running and fast-running speeds.

Unless you are a crack shot and have practiced shooting at fast-moving targets at a variety of distances, you will be a much more effective and humane deer hunter if you limit your shots at running deer to only those that can be taken at close range where the required lead is minimal.

The greatest challenge of deer hunting is to hunt in such a way that you are in a position to take close shots at deer that are standing still or walking slowly. This may require more hunting skill, but developing the ability to get within close range of unsuspecting deer is what deer hunting should be about.

RANGE (YDS.)	DEER'S FORWARD SPEED (MPH)	REQUIRED LEAD (INCHES)
50	10	12
50	20	25
75	10	20
75	20	38
100	10	28
100	20	52

Trailing Wounded Deer

I DO NOT SUBSCRIBE to the often-stated recommendation to sit down and wait a half hour before trailing a deer that was hit and ran off after the shot. Although it is true that waiting before you trail the deer will give the animal time to die or become immobilized before you approach it, waiting also provides time for another hunter to find your deer and claim it before you do. This is especially true if you are hunting on heavily pressured public land.

Don't be discouraged if you don't find your deer right away. Keep going in the direction the deer was headed when you last saw it, and check all thick places carefully. When hit, deer head for heavy cover.

When you shoot, watch the deer as far as you can and mentally mark the spot where it disappeared. Now, mark the spot you shot from with a strip of surveyor's tape. Next, reload your rifle, put it on safety, and walk to the spot where you last saw the deer. If you can't see the downed deer, mark that spot by tying a strip of surveyor's tape to an overhead branch and search the ground for blood, hair or tracks. Continue in the direction in which the deer was traveling, moving slowly and scanning ahead for a sight of the deer while searching the ground for signs.

A deer shot through the lungs, heart, or liver may drop in its tracks or run at full speed until the blood supply to its brain decreases and the animal piles up wherever it is. Usually, the deer tumbles into a hollow in the ground and is found stretched out in the open. But on several occasions I have had a hard time finding bucks that fell dead within 100 yards of where I shot them because they fell into holes or leaped into heavy cover in their mad rush to escape.

I well remember a 10-pointer that I shot when he came to my rattling horns. When I fired, he was standing broadside no more than 40 yards away, and my crosshairs were settled tight behind his shoulder, halfway between the top of his back and the bottom of his chest. "Dead!" I said to myself, as he hunched up and bounded off after the shot.

I walked to where the buck had been standing and looked in the direction in which he ran. Nothing. I checked the ground for hair and blood and found neither. Moving off in the direction he had taken, I found the ground was frozen hard and his tracks indistinguishable. I expected to find him within 100 yards or so, but did not. Nor could I find any trace of blood or hair along my route. Ahead lay a thicket of young firs and spruces with interlacing branches. Only by lying on my stomach was I able to view the ground beneath them.

After nearly an hour of pacing methodically back and forth through the thick woods, I still had not found my deer. Still, I was positive my shot had been good and that he must be lying dead somewhere close by.

After another fruitless half hour I was completely frustrated. I was tempted to think that I had missed. Only the fact that I had experienced this sort of frustration before, yet finally found my deer, made me persist.

USE YOUR NOSE

Suddenly, I smelled him. The musky smell of a buck in the rut is unmistakable. You smell it instantly when you walk up to a dead deer, and I smelled it then. Turning to face the soft breeze that bore the scent to me, I crawled forward into the densest part of the thicket and within a few yards came to a deep depression that was totally obscured by overlapping fir branches that drooped close to the ground. My buck lay dead in the depression, with not even the wide curve of his big rack showing above the ground. He had run that far, leaped into the thicket, and fallen dead in the one spot where he could not be seen.

That is not the only time I have found dead deer by smelling them, and I recommend using your nose as well as your eyes when searching for a deer you know was hit.

MODERN BULLETS MAY NOT EXIT

Modern bullets are designed to lose all of their force inside a big-game animal, so they often do not exit. The lack of a large exit wound considerably reduces the amount of blood a deer spills and makes trailing a wounded deer that much more difficult. Bullet manufacturers say that modern bullets deliver such a high degree of shocking power that more deer are killed in their tracks with no trailing necessary, but the fact is that when you do hit a deer that runs off but does not spill blood, trailing it can be a real challenge.

Even deer that may be suffering enormous internal bleeding sometimes spill little blood. Fat layers often plug the small bullet entry wound and prevent much blood from being lost. Deer that are shot through the lungs lose blood through their mouth and nose, but deer shot in the heart, liver, or spinal column may lose very little blood before they fall.

CHECK THE THICK SPOTS

A deer that is mortally wounded may run uphill or downhill or stay on the level. It may go anywhere, but if it is hit badly enough to have to stop, it will head for the thickest cover it can find. Knowing this, pay close attention to any heavy cover that may hide it, and search those places closely if you do not have a blood trail leading you to its location.

Carry your rifle with the safety on, but in a position from which you can mount it quickly for a close shot. If your rifle is equipped with a variable-power telescopic sight, set it on the lowest magnification in order to have the widest possible field of view if the deer should suddenly jump up close to you and begin to run.

You should find a clump of hair at the spot where the deer was hit. There may or may not be blood at that place, depending on whether or not the bullet passed through the deer's body. The blood trail usually begins a few yards down the deer's escape route. Skidding tracks indicate that the deer was hit hard and is disoriented. If the deer falls, it leaves torn earth and scattered leaves. Bright, frothy blood implies a lung shot; you can expect to find the deer dead not far down the trail. Dark, blackish blood suggests that the deer was hit in the paunch. It will die, but not for a while. Right now, it will head for heavy cover. Bits of bone may be from the lower leg. A deer hit there can go a long way.

As you move along the trail, be careful not to step on the deer's tracks or spots where blood or hair is found. Walk beside the signs, not on them. You may have to go back over a portion of the trail if you lose it, and it may prove impossible to do so if you have disturbed the signs.

Mark the Trail

If you have only a sparse blood trail to follow, mark the trail with bits of surveyor's tape as you go so that you can always return to the last blood spot when you have difficulty finding the next one. If you fail to find the deer by the end of the day, you will have an easier time finding the trail again the next morning if you have marked it well. (After you either find your deer or are forced to abandon the trail, go back and remove the surveyor's tape marks because they may create confusion for others who find them later.)

Follow Up Every Shot

Don't be discouraged if you don't find your deer right away. If you feel the shot was good, you probably have a deer down, and it is up to you to find it. If there is snow on the ground or if the deer is bleeding heavily, you won't have any trouble following its trail. It is when the ground is bare and frozen hard and the deer has stopped bleeding that the trail becomes hard to read.

All you can do in those situations is to keep going in the direction in which the deer was headed and search hardest in the thickest places. If you are hunting with one or more partners, call them for assistance. Separate yourselves at a distance that allows you to see the ground clearly between you, and then move through the woods abreast.

If the deer travels a long distance and you have not caught up with it by day's end, mark the spot clearly and return the next morning to follow the trail again. It is very likely that you will find the deer wherever it bedded for the night. If the ground is cold, the meat of a dead deer that has lain out overnight will not be spoiled.

If in the end you are forced to abandon the trail without finding the deer, ask yourself what went wrong, and try to avoid making that mistake in the future. Most deer that are wounded but get away are the result of hunters taking long shots at running targets. Close shots at standing or walking deer usually result in dead deer where you can find them within a few minutes.

Field Dressing Your Deer

DEER RARELY FALL in a place that is suitable for field dressing the carcass. They tumble into hollows in the ground or fall in thick cover where you will be too confined to field dress the deer properly. To make field dressing easier, you want your deer out in the open on raised ground where you can stretch out the carcass. So, before you get out your knife, drag the deer to an open place on level or gently sloping ground. Place it so the deer's head is either on the level or slightly uphill. If possible, place large rocks or logs beside the deer's shoulders to prevent the carcass from rolling.

You Don't Need a Big Knife

A large knife is not necessary. Knives with 3½-inch blades are ample. If you are using a folding knife, choose one with a locking blade that will not fold up on your fingers while you are using it.

Some hunters begin by removing the deer's tarsal scent glands from the inside of the hind legs in order to prevent the spread of the strong, musky scent to the meat. I do not recommend doing this, however, because removing the glands gets the scent on your hands, so that the scent is transmitted to every part of the deer you touch. I prefer to leave the scent glands in place and avoid touching them. The scent will not spread from the glands if they do not come into contact with the deer's flesh. They will come off cleanly with the hide when the deer is skinned at home.

Once you have the deer firmly positioned on its back, cut around the scrotum, detach the testicles and penis, and throw them away from the carcass. If the deer is a female, remove the udder and throw it away.

Next, find the soft spot at the base of the chest, just below the ribs, and make a small 2-inch cut through the skin and into the cavity. Straddle the carcass, facing the animal's tail. If you hold the knife in your right hand, put the first two fingers of your left hand into the incision you have made. Turn your knife so that the cutting edge is up. Slip the point of your knife blade between the two fingers that are inside the carcass. Don't let the blade tip extend into the body cavity and nick the organs. With the tip of the blade protected between your fingers, push both hands forward, with your left-hand fingertips advancing just ahead of the blade. This action will cause the blade to cut through the skin and belly lining from the inside while your fingers prevent the blade from touching the organs. Cut all the way to the pelvis in this manner.

Now, turn and straddle the carcass, facing the head, and get ready to open the chest cavity.

Splitting the breastbone, or sternum, is not necessary. This 2-inch wide, 10-inch long piece of cartilage can be completely removed a lot easier than it can be split; once it is out of the way, you will have a wide opening into which you can reach with both hands to free the lungs, heart, windpipe, and esophagus.

To remove the sternum, split the skin that covers it all the way up to the base of the throat. Next, peel the skin and the thin layer of flesh under it back about an inch from each side of the sternum to expose the points where the ribs join the sternum. These joints are soft "buttons" that you can easily cut with your knife.

Once you have exposed the sternum, cut through the "buttons" on each side of it. Then grasp the base of the sternum with one hand and pull up. The sternum will break off at the throat end. Cut it off and toss it away. You now have a broad opening from the pelvis all the way to the throat. Reach into the throat and cut through the windpipe and esophagus and pull them out of the carcass.

Now roll the carcass on its side and scoop out the intestines and stomach onto the ground. Next, use your knife to free the lungs and heart, and cut through the diaphragm membrane that separates the chest cavity from the body cavity. Pull these organs out onto the ground as well. The carcass is now empty, but the large intestine is still attached through the pelvic opening to the rectum. Turn the carcass on its belly to let the blood drain out of the open cavity. Once it is drained, turn it on its back again.

With the knife held in your right hand and the tip of the blade protected between the fingers of your left hand, you can cut through the skin and belly lining from the inside without having the blade touch the organs.

To remove the sternum (or breastbone), peel the skin back to expose the points where the ribs join the sternum. Then cut through these "buttons" with your knife while pulling up on the sternum with your free hand. When the "buttons" are cut, the sternum will break loose and can be thrown away, exposing a wide opening to the interior of the chest.

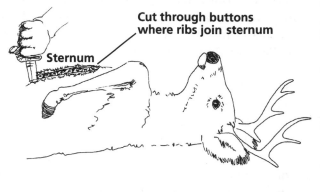

Cut through buttons where ribs join sternum

Sternum

Turn the carcass on its side and scoop out the intestines and stomach on to the ground, leaving the large intestine attached through the pelvic opening to the rectum. Use your knife to cut through the diaphragm and free all remaining organs.

Make a circular cut through the skin around the rectum to free it from the carcass without cutting the intestine. Tie off the exposed section of intestine with a short piece of string. Next, use your knife to free the intestine from the pelvic wall. Gently pull the intestine and rectum through the pelvis from the belly side.

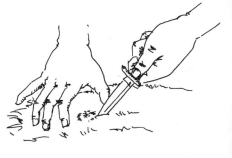

Use the point of your knife to make a circular cut through the skin around the rectum to free it from the carcass without cutting the intestine. When the rectum is free, hold it with your left hand and push your knife blade full length into the pelvic opening outside the intestine to free the intestine from the pelvic walls. Then pull the rectum and a few inches of the attached intestine outside the carcass and tie it off with a short piece of string. This precaution will prevent excrement from emerging from the intestine later. Now, push your knife into the pelvic opening from the belly side, and gently probe the outside of the intestine within the pelvic wall as you pull gently on the intestine from the point where it enters the pelvis. The freed intestine, with the intact bladder attached, will pull through. Try not to spill the bladder's urine contents on the carcass. If it does spill, wash the urine away as soon as possible.

Pull the carcass a few feet away from the gut pile, turn it on its belly, and let it drain while you wash your hands with water or snow. Now drag the carcass to the nearest water and rinse out the body cavity as thoroughly as possible. A well-washed carcass will be much more happily received at home.

You've completed your hunt, you have your deer, and it's dressed and ready to drag out of the woods. Now the work begins!

Dragging Your Deer Home

BEFORE YOU BEGIN dragging your deer home, make sure you know where you are. Take a break. Locate yourself on your map and plan a route out of the woods. The best route is not always a straight shot back to your vehicle or camp. Study the terrain and choose a route that will be downhill as much as possible. Avoid swamps.

Dragging a deer out of the woods is never easy, but there is one way that is less taxing than all others. You'll need a six-foot piece of rope. Make the drag rope a permanent part of your deer-hunting outfit and carry it with you every time you go out.

Tie one end of the rope around the base of the deer's antlers, or around its neck, just behind the ears, if it is antlerless. Then wrap the rope once around the muzzle in a half hitch so that you will be pulling the deer directly from that point rather than from the antlers. This will help to keep the deer's head from tangling in brush as you go.

Now, search around and find a 2-foot-long stick about 2 inches thick. The wood should be cured, not rotten. Tie the free end of the rope in the center of the piece of wood. This is your draw bar. The wooden draw bar will be much more comfortable to pull on than the rough deer's antlers, and you will not have to lift the deer's forequarters when you pull.

Grip the wooden draw bar at both ends with your hands held behind you and throw your weight into the effort as you begin to pull. Lean forward as you progress so that your weight does the pulling, not just your arms.

A wooden draw bar is much more comfortable to pull on than the rough edges of a deer's antlers, and you will not have to lift the deer's forequarters when you pull.

From time to time the carcass will become snagged on something—a log, saplings, a blowdown, whatever gets in the way. Try to avoid these kinds of obstacles, although the deer will probably snag anyway.

When the deer gets caught, turn around to face it and pull backwards, using your arms to lift the deer's head when necessary. It may help to shorten the rope by wrapping it around the wooden draw bar a few times and tying it with a half hitch when lifting is required.

If you have a helper, you may want to use a somewhat longer draw bar—say 3 feet. Each person grasps a side with one hand and you pull together shoulder to shoulder. Having a helper makes the job more than twice as easy, so don't hesitate to call for help if you can.

TAKE YOUR TIME

Don't try to hurry when you are dragging a deer. Take time to rest along the way, and don't be in a rush to get out of the woods. Accidents happen when you are tired and pushing your limits. Take it easy and enjoy your success. The hunt is just a memory now, so make it a good one.

CHAPTER

Firearms Safety

THERE IS NEVER AN EXCUSE for a hunting accident. Every hunting accident that has ever occurred could have been prevented if simple firearms safety rules had been followed.

When hunting accidents occur, the nonhunting public blames all of us who own and use firearms. Ensure that you are always a safe hunter and do everything you can to promote firearms safety. It is never "cool" to be casual with firearms.

If every hunter obeyed the following firearms safety rules, hunting accidents would never happen.

The author poses with a North Country buck. The only good hunter is a safe one. Always follow basic firearms safety rules.

1. Treat every firearm as if it is loaded.
2. Whenever you pick up a firearm, open the action and check to see if it is loaded.
3. Never point a firearm at anything you would not intend to shoot.
4. Never take the safety off until you have positively identified your target.
5. Never use your rifle's telescopic sight to "scope" a person or an animal you do not intend to shoot.
6. Keep guns and ammunition out of the reach of children.
7. Do not mix guns and alcohol or drugs.
8. Unload your gun before climbing a fence or other obstruction.
9. Be sure you are using the right ammo for your gun.
10. *Treat every firearm as if it is loaded.*

These are pretty simple rules, and if we all followed them, absolute firearms safety would be achieved. Do your best to make that happen.

Remember, the only good hunter is a safe one.

Hunting Gear Checklist

Before going into the woods, be sure you are carrying the following:

- Hunting license and deer tag
- String to attach tag to deer
- Rifle
- Ammo
- Compass
- Map
- Knife
- Drag rope
- Matches or lighter
- Emergency rain jacket
- Aluminum emergency blanket
- Flashlight with fresh batteries
- Lunch and energy bar
- Water

CHAPTER

Favorite Venison Recipes

YOU CAN'T BUY meat that is better for you than venison from wild deer. The animals have not been fed growth hormones or artificial fatteners; they eat only healthy, natural foods. Furthermore, deer grow fat in a layer that can be removed in the butchering process, yielding flavorful red meat that is extremely low in cholesterol.

Following are some of my favorite venison recipes. I hope you get a deer this season so you can give them a try!

Steaks, roasts, and stew meat from older deer will be more tender and flavorful if they are marinated as follows for 24 hours before cooking:

Marinade

1 bottle red wine	3 garlic cloves, crushed
1 cup balsamic vinegar	3 cloves
1 cup olive oil	1 teaspoon crushed peppercorns
2 teaspoons salt	2 bay leaves, crushed
3 medium onions, sliced	1 sprig fresh thyme

Combine the ingredients in a deep dish and add any large cut of venison. Let the meat marinate for 24 hours in a cool place, turning it occasionally. The marinade may be refrigerated and used again.

Pan-Seared Loin (Backstrap) of Venison

Cut a venison backstrap into 8-inch sections and trim away all fat and ligaments. Heat a black iron skillet lightly rubbed with olive oil. Add the meat and sear it on both sides until it is browned on the outside but rare or medium rare inside. Remove the meat and let it rest on a cutting board. While the meat is resting, assemble the following ingredients:

1 cup Bovril or beef bouillon	1 shallot, chopped
½ cup balsamic vinegar	1 tablespoon grated orange peel
½ cup red wine	1 sprig fresh rosemary
1 tablespoon green peppercorns	

1. Quickly sauté the shallot and peppercorns in the olive oil still in the skillet. Add the wine and vinegar to deglaze the skillet. Add the beef bouillon and simmer while stirring until an appealing thickness is achieved. At the last minute, add the grated orange peel and the rosemary.

2. Angle the knife and slice the meat into ½-inch slices. Arrange the slices on a serving dish and pour the sauce over them just before serving. Excellent served with a green salad and puréed butternut squash.

Camp-Style Pan-Seared Venison Steak

Slice ½-inch-thick steaks from the backstraps, upper hind leg, or rump of a deer. Trim away the external fat and connective tissue. Scatter ¼ teaspoon of salt in the bottom of a hot iron skillet. Lay the steaks in the skillet and sear on both sides for 1 to 2 minutes, turning only once. Serve rare or medium rare, hot from the skillet, with mashed potatoes and a green salad.

Venison Pot Roast

This recipe is so simple it sounds dull. Believe me, it makes the best pot roast and gravy you've ever tasted.

3- to 5 pound chunk of boned meat from hind leg or neck of a deer	1 cup water
1 can beer	1 package dried onion soup mix
	1 can cream of mushroom soup

1. On top of the stove, sear the meat in a deep, heavy, hot, oiled pot until all sides are browned. Add the beer, water, dried onion soup mix, and cream of mushroom soup. Reduce the heat, cover the pot, and simmer for 3 to 4 hours.

2. Remove the meat from the pot and slice it thinly. Add water to the pot if needed to achieve a smooth gravy. Return the meat slices to the gravy and serve with mashed potatoes and a green salad.

Venison Hamburger

Meat from the shoulders and lower legs should be used for stew meat or ground for hamburger. Here's how to make really good venison hamburger.

1. Trim away and discard all fat and connective tissues, leaving only lean meat. Cut the meat into 2-inch cubes.

2. Dice strips of smoked bacon into half-inch squares and mix with venison cubes at a ratio of 1 pound of bacon to 10 pounds of venison. Run mixture through a meat grinder two times.

3. Grill, broil or fry as hamburger patties, or use in any recipe that calls for ground meat.

Old-Fashioned Deer Stew

2 pounds cubed venison from shoulder, shanks, or neck	1 quart beef bouillon
2 tablespoons vegetable oil	2 tablespoons potato starch dissolved in ½ cup cold water
1 medium onion	2 cups cubed potatoes
1 teaspoon dried thyme	1 cup carrots cut into 1½-inch pieces
2 bay leaves	1 cup small white onions
1 cup red wine	

1. Sear the venison cubes in a heavy skillet or large pot over high heat in 2 tablespoons of oil. Deglaze the pan with the wine. Add the broth, herbs, and onions.

2. Simmer for 2 hours, then remove the bay leaves (they can cause injury if swallowed). Add the vegetables and simmer for ½ hour more. Thicken the liquid with potato starch. Garnish with chopped parsley and serve.

European Venison Ragout

2½ pounds venison in 2-inch cubes	¼ cup flour
6 slices bacon cut into 2-inch pieces	2 cups sliced onions
2 cups beef bouillon	2 cups sliced carrots
1½ cups red wine or 12 ounces beer	1 cup sliced or whole mushrooms
3 tablespoons brandy	1 small can (14½ ounces) diced tomatoes
1½ teaspoons dried thyme or sage	

1 bay leaf	2 cloves garlic
¼ teaspoon ground black pepper	1 strip orange peel, 1 by 4 inches

1. Marinate the venison in the wine or beer, brandy, herbs, and vegetables 3 to 6 hours. Remove the venison cubes and drain, reserving the marinade. Fry the bacon pieces in a skillet and transfer them to a large casserole. In the reserved fat in the skillet, brown the drained venison cubes. Transfer the meat to the casserole and add ¼ cup of flour to the drippings in the skillet.

2. Cook, stirring, until the flour is golden. Stir in the reserved marinade. Pour the mixture over the meat in the casserole. Add the vegetables, cover, and bake 2½ to 3 hours at 350 degrees.

Venison Chili with Beer

2 pounds venison cut into ½-inch cubes, or ground	2 tablespoons chili powder
12 ounces beer	1 teaspoon ground coriander
4 large onions, chopped fine	½ teaspoon ground cumin
2 cloves garlic, chopped fine	½ cup tomato paste
½ cup vegetable oil	1½ teaspoons salt
	1 cup water, more if needed

Simmer the onions and garlic in the oil until soft and translucent. Add the venison and toss with a fork until well done. Add the remaining ingredients and mix thoroughly. Simmer for 1 hour, adding water to maintain proper consistency. Serve with rice and beans.

Venison Spaghetti Sauce

1 pound ground venison	1 large bottle tomato-based spaghetti sauce
2 tablespoons vegetable oil	1 pound vermicelli or linguine

Cook the venison in the vegetable oil in a heavy skillet until well done, breaking it up with a fork as it cooks. Add the spaghetti sauce and mix well. Simmer until hot, and serve with the pasta, which has been boiled in a separate large pot until tender.

Index

Accidents, 105
Aiming, at deer, 89 90
Air currents, 49
Antlerless deer
  seasons, 3-4
  vocalization of, 58
Antlers, 4-6
  rattling of, 22, 62-69
  rubs, 35 36
Autumn, feeding during, 27-28, 45-46

Backstrap, venison (recipe), 109
Backtracks, 22, 42
Balch, Alfred, 51
Bedding sites, 22, 24-25
Big buck country, 7-10
Big country hunting, 66
Binoculars, 13
Birds, 14
Bleat calls, 61
Blood trails, 96
Blowdown, 35
Blowing. See Snorting
Boats, 8 9
Bolt-action rifles, 77
Bow hunting, 46
Breeding season. See Rut
Brush busters, 77
Bucks. See also Deer
  antler-rattling and, 67-68
  bedding down, 22
  dominant, 6, 13-14, 36-37, 39

droppings, 19
fighting, 34-35, 62, 63, 65-66
groups of, 13-14
location, 7-10
ratio to does, 3
during rut, 34-39, 95
size, 4
subdominant, 13-14, 67
tracks, 17-19
traveling patterns, 19, 28, 34
urination, 19
vocalization, 58
Bullets, 77-79
  exit of, 95
  placement of, 81-82
  trajectories, 77-79, 85-86, 88

Canoes, 8-9
Carcasses
  dragging, 102-103
  field dressing, 98-101
Chili, venison (recipe), 111
Clothing, 31-33
Cold weather, 25
Compass, use of, 72, 74-75
Crops, deer and, 46
Crosshairs, 83

Deer. See also Antlerless deer; Bucks;
  Does
  activity of, 25, 26, 27-28
  aiming at, 89-90

Deer *(continued)*
  bedding down, 11, 13, 24–25
  dead. *See* Carcasses
  feeding, 27–28, 45–46
  field dressing, 98–101
  lungs, 89
  movements, 14–16
  nocturnal habits, 26–27
  population balance, 1–3, 4
  resting, 11, 13
  running, 90–92
  seeing, 11–16
  shooting, 89–92
  tracks, 17–23
  traveling patterns, 45
  vocalization, 58
  weather and, 20, 24–30
  wounded, 93–97
Deer calls, 58–59
Dewclaws, 17, 18, 20
Direction
  keeping track of, 73
Does. *See also* Antlerless deer; Deer
  antler-rattling and, 67
  droppings, 19
  during estrus, 36–37, 55–56
  harvesting of, 3–4
  ratio to bucks, 3
  tracks, 18–19
  traveling patterns, 19, 28
  urination, 19, 55–56
  vocalization, 58
Drag marks, of bucks, 18
Drag ropes, 102
Draw bars, 102–103
Dress, for hunting, 31–33
Drives, 40
Droppings, 19
Duplex reticles, 83

"Engine room," 89–90
Estrus, 36–37, 55–56. *See also* Rut

Fawns. *See also* Antlerless deer
  vocalization of, 58
Feeding locations, 37, 45–46
Field dressing, of deer, 98–101

Firearms safety, 105–106
Flat-shooting calibers, 77

Gear, for hunting, 107
Global positioning systems, 75
Groups
  of bucks, 13–14
  hunting in, 40–42
Grunt calls, 22, 59–60
Grunt-snort combinations, 58, 60, 65

Hamburger, venison (recipe), 110
Henry, Jim, 25
Hills, 9

Knives, 98
Knockdown power, 78–79
Knocking on wood, 61

Lakes, 8–9
Landmarks, 72, 74
Lever-action rifles, 76
Loin, of venison (recipe), 109
Lungs, of deer, 89

Maps
  scale of, 70–71
  topographic, 43, 70–72
Marinade, for venison (recipe), 108
Moonlight, 26–27
Movements
  of birds and animals, 14
  of deer, 14–16
  of hunter, 52–54. *See also* Still-hunting

Native Americans, 40
Noisemaking, 40

Open sights, 80

Pairs, hunting in, 42
Peep sights, 81, 87
Polypropylene, 33
Popcorn days, 29–30
Post-and-crosshair reticles, 83
Pot roast, venison (recipe), 109–110
Pump-action rifles, 77

Radios, 42–44
Ragout, venison (recipe), 110–111
Rain, 29
Rattling, of antlers, 22, 62–69
Receiver/peep sights, 87
Recipes, 108–111
Reticles, 83
Rifles
    bolt-action, 77
    lever-action, 76
    pump-action, 77
    semiautomatic, 77
    sighting-in, 84–88
    sights, 80–83
Rivers, 8–9
Rubs
    of antlers, 21, 35–36
Rut. *See also* Estrus
    antler-rattling during, 62
    buck behavior during, 34–39, 59–60,
        62, 95
    tracks during, 18, 19
    vocalization during, 59–60

Scent
    of bucks, 95
    estrus and, 37, 38
    human, 25, 48–49, 51–52, 56–57
    use in hunting, 55–57
Scrapes, 21, 37–38, 55, 56
Seeing deer, 11–16
Shooting, of deer, 89–92
Sights
    metallic, 88
    open, 80, 88
    peep, 81, 87
    receiver/peep, 87
    telescopic, 81–83, 86–87, 96
Snorting, 58. *See also* Grunt-snort com-
    binations
Snow, 20, 29
Soaps
    scent-eradicating, 57

Spaghetti sauce, venison (recipe), 111
Spoor, 19
Stands, hunting from, 45–50, 66
Steaks, venison (recipe), 109
Stew, deer (recipe), 110
Still-hunting, 41, 42, 51–54
Storms, 24–25
Sunlight
    hunting in, 29, 53
Swamps, 9

Telescopic sights, 13, 81–83, 86–87, 96
Time
    keeping track of, 73
Topographic maps, 43
Tracks, 17–23, 66
    blood, 96
    size of, 20–21
    weather and, 20
Trajectories, of bullets, 77–79, 85–86
Trees, 9–10
    stands in, 45–50, 66
Trophy racks. *See* Antlers

Unfocusing eyes, 14
Urination
    of bucks, 19, 38
    of does, 19, 55–56
U.S. Geological Survey, 70–71

Variable scopes, 82–83, 96
Venison recipes, 108–111
Voice-calling, 58–59

Water. *See* Lakes; Rivers
Weather, 24–30
    tracks and, 20
Whitetail deer. *See* Deer
Wind
    direction, 22, 48–49, 51–52
    hunting and, 25, 28
Woods, 9–10